On teaching classics

On teaching classics

J. E. Sharwood Smith

University of London
Institute of Education

Routledge & Kegan Paul
London, Henley and Boston

WITHDRAWN
NORTHEASTERN ILLINOIS
UNIVERSITY LIBRARY

First published in 1977
by Routledge & Kegan Paul Ltd
39 Store Street,
London WC1E 7DD,
Broadway House,
Newtown Road,
Henley-on-Thames,
Oxon RG9 1EN and
9 Park Street,
Boston, Mass. 02108, USA
Set in IBM Press Roman by
Express Litho Service (Oxford)
and printed in Great Britain by
Redwood Burn Ltd
Trowbridge and Esher

British Library Cataloguing in Publication Data

Sharwood Smith, John

On teaching classics – (Students library
of education).

1. Greek language – Study and teaching (Secondary)
– Great Britain   2. Greek literature – Study and
teaching (Secondary) – Great Britain   3. Latin
language – Study and teaching (Secondary) – Great
Britain   4. Latin literature – Study and teaching
(Secondary) – Great Britain

I. Title II. Series
880'.07'1241   PA 78.G7
ISBN 0 7100 8580 X

The Students Library of Education has been designed to meet the needs of students of Education at Colleges of Education and at University Institutes and Departments. It will also be valuable for practising teachers and educationists. The series takes full account of the latest developments in teacher-training and of new methods and approaches in education. Separate volumes will provide authoritative and up-to-date accounts of the topics within the major fields of sociology, philosophy and history of education, educational psychology and method. Care has been taken that specialist topics are treated lucidly and usefully for the non-specialist reader. Altogether, the Students Library of Education will provide a comprehensive introduction and guide to anyone concerned with the study of education, and with educational theory and practice.

To Michael Gunningham and all those who have contributed from their skills, their experience and their scholarship to the achievements of JACT. To them this book owes everything.

Contents

Contents

Chapter one

Prologue

On nomenclature, definitions and obsolescence

No doubt many subjects have had problems of identity and definition, even before the sociologists began asking awkward questions about the social basis of knowledge. There can be few teachers of Classics who have not at some time been embarrassed and perplexed to explain their role in life to a casually met stranger unacquainted with the academic world. It has been said, not without reason, that Classics is not so much a subject as an ideology. The ancestry of the words 'Classics' and 'classical' makes an interesting study, but one that is beyond the scope of this little book; nor is there space to review the traditions of classical education, which were prefigured by the sophists, given form in the Hellenistic world, adopted by the Romans, preserved in mutilated form throughout the Dark and Middle Ages, to be revived in the educational programmes of the Humanists; and, finally, after a period of degeneracy, reinvigorated by Arnold of Rugby and his fellow reformers. Present-day practices and present-day prejudices could be illuminated by such a study and such a review, but it must suffice here to say that if any shred of mystique (or taint of infamy) still clings to the name *Classics* – or even to the subject *Latin* – this derives from an aristocratic ideal. This ideal was associated with a myth. The myth was that of the effortless superiority of the classically educated man, able, by virtue of his training, to master any problem in any sphere of life so long as it was amenable to intellectual analysis (and what problem of any significance – so went the myth – was not?). The myth bore this relation to reality, that, at a time when most able boys were given a classical education, a large number of very able men could be shown to have been trained in Classics. It had other, more disputable, connections with reality which will be discussed later, but the efficacy of the myth was destroyed (if by nothing else) by the advances in Science and in scientific education, which revealed that good administrators could be created otherwise than through a study of Classics, and that in some spheres of public activity even an alpha mind was no compensation for ignorance of Science.

To be brief and brutal, idealization of Classics was often based on snobbery, just as prejudice against Classics is now frequently based on counter-snobbery. Unfortunately for the present public image of Classics, Hellenistic culture *was* anti-popular, and so is most of the literature transmitted through classical education. Many classical scholars have, over the past century, deplored the advent of full democracy, many anti-populists have found support for their views in Greek and Roman literature; and, at school level, elementary Latin was used long before the invention of IQ tests — and long after — as an instrument of selection for an intellectual élite; while at the same time the institutionalized pre-eminence of Classics played some part in keeping the upper classes on top.

Now that technological and social change have rendered obsolete the domination of a small social and intellectual élite trained in a literary culture, it seems probable that classical education, as once given to our Victorian and Edwardian forebears, and as still given to a very small minority of the secondary school population, is equally obsolete. Does this mean that the study of the Greek and Latin languages, the study of the surviving literatures of Greece and Rome, of the social, political, economic history of Graeco-Roman civilization, and the study of its art and architecture, are also, individually and collectively, obsolete? Any attempt to answer this question must wait until the reader has considered the nature and potentialities of several aspects of classical learning. But first a brief discussion of the definition and scope of 'Classics', so-called.

A definition

There have been many attempts to define 'Classics'. Of those I know I find the following — which has the powerful authority of Ulrich von Wilamowitz-Moellendorf — the most useful for the purpose of discussion.

> Philology which still keeps the label 'classical' — although it no longer claims for itself the pre-eminence implied in that appellation — is determined by its object, namely Graeco-Roman culture in its essential nature and in all the manifestations of its life. This culture is a unity, even if sharp boundaries cannot be given to its beginning or to its end. The task or purpose of philology is through the power of Science (Wissenschaft) to make that past life live again: the song of the poet, the thought of the philosopher and the lawgiver, the

holiness of the temple and the sentiments of believer and unbeliever, the multiple and varied activity of the market-place and port, land and sea, and men at their work and at their play. . . . Because the life which we strive to know is a unity, our science itself is a unity.

This, it should be observed, is a scholar's definition of classical scholarship, not an educationist's definition of classical education; and it is instructive to note how much less comprehensive the latter has always been in England — and indeed, though to a less extent, in Germany also — and how increasingly less comprehensive it became as it yielded more and more to the insistence of other subjects for the dismemberment of its empire over the curriculum.

The Victorian classical education was basically linguistic, but at its upper levels it blossomed out into literary, historical and philosophical study. Plato, Thucydides, Homer and the Attic tragedians were its main goals in Greek; Horace, Virgil, Livy and Cicero in Latin. What the majority of pupils, who never got beyond the lower levels, encountered was a great deal of translating English into Latin and sometimes, but not always, Greek; and rather less of construing Ovid, Horace, Virgil, and possibly Xenophon, and some easier passages of Plato and Thucydides. What they did not encounter was 'the thought of the lawgiver', 'the holiness of the temple' and 'the multiple and varied activity of the market-place and port', nor did they encounter (what Wilamowitz does not mention, but is as surely a part of Graeco-Roman culture as its literature) the activities of the Greeks and Romans in art, architecture and engineering.

Two of Wilamowitz's phrases beg further consideration:

1. 'Graeco-Roman culture in its essential form.'

As the claims of other subjects have, in the schools, subtracted more and more time from the classics, there have been attempts to identify the *essence* of Graeco-Roman culture — sometimes referred to as 'central Classics'. Cicero and Virgil have been put forward as candidates for this centrality. In my opinion the search for a small core of central study is a vain one. What scholars have in the past selected for study, and what anyone is likely to select today as 'central Classics', reveals — not the essence of the Graeco-Roman past — but contemporary preoccupations. It seems to me unhistorical to suppose that a civilization which lasted for one thousand years of constant, and sometimes violent, change can be reduced to an essential epitome.

2. 'This culture is a unity.'

This statement needs qualification. Classical education has, in the past, given a spurious appearance of unity to Graeco-Roman antiquity by creating out of it an educational programme. There is a real unity in the

3

study of any one of the societies which in the aggregate make up the millennium of Greek and Roman history: Athens of the fifth century, the Hellenistic world, Rome of the late Republic and of the Early Empire, to give some obvious examples. In these the student can see how the phenomena of culture interact upon one another. A unity linking the age that produced geometric pottery to the age of St Augustine, or, to draw the limits more closely, a unity linking Peisistratus to Hadrian, would be a much more artificial concept.

This question of unity is important because, if respect for any such overall unity were conceived as an essential feature of the study of the ancient world, this would invalidate all autonomous courses in Greek Literature in Translation, in Ancient History, in Greek Drama, in Paganism and Christianity in the Ancient World – all of which, together with others like them, will be discussed in later chapters. It would also invalidate all classical studies below graduate level undertaken now or in the past. Never has a unified study of all the cultural phenomena listed by Wilamowitz been pursued as a part of general education.

Any serious educator – that is, a teacher who is not content to teach merely what is in the syllabus for the reason that it *is* in the syllabus – will want to help his pupils to learn how to live. Study of the Graeco-Roman world has in the past been used – at times passionately – for this purpose. If it is to earn a place in the education of the future it must be so used again. Put into mundane terms this means that, for example, Thucydides must be studied not merely to discover the style and content of his history, but why he wrote history and what is the nature of the history that he wrote; pupils must not merely construe Virgil but understand his poetry and the circumstances which caused him to write what and as he did. Not only must it be asked when the Parthenon was built, by whom and what did it look like, but what was its purpose, or purposes, in the widest possible sense – in the way that one might ask the purpose of Sydney Opera House, the Houses of Parliament and St Peter's Basilica in Rome and not be satisfied with the answer that they are for ticket-holders to hear opera performed, for Members of Parliament to make laws in, and for Roman Catholics to worship God in.

If Classics is to help people to live, then a great many questions must be asked of the Ancient World, to which answers can be discovered (partial answers, of course; total answers not being available to the human condition) that will shed light on the choices perennially open to human beings and to human societies in the conduct of their affairs.

The reader must reach his own conclusions about the obsolescence or perenniality of Classics in education, but a simile may be appropriate. The simile likens Classical antiquity to a capacious attic, rather difficult of access but rewarding to visit. It contains many intellectual and aesthetic heirlooms; some of recognized value, others no more than interesting bric-à-brac. A few of the best pieces were taken down by the family long ago and are still in constant use, together with a fair amount of the bric-à-brac. In the past each generation has developed different tastes and different needs from its predecessor's, and there has there-fore been a certain amount of toing and froing to the attic to relegate once cherished articles which subsequently fell into contempt. In the course of the toing and froing other fascinating objects have been un-covered which have been found to answer the new needs and to appeal to the new tastes. Of course, in the meantime, many other members of the family have been busy adding contemporary artefacts to the family's possessions; not all of which have ended up a generation later in the dustbin or the Furniture Depository. So, over the years, the family home has become more than adequately furnished, and the questions to be faced are: what should be relegated without more ado, what can usefully be kept in service, and are there things lying unconsidered in the attic that could be of significance to this or the next generation?

On teaching classical civilization to the lower and middle forms of the secondary school

... in the transmission of the 'Legacy of Greece', the Renaissance use of popular translations in popular education – the chained copy of North's 'Plutarch' in the village church, alongside the Authorized Version, as you may see it at Bicester today – gave place to the strict 'classical education' of the public schools and older universities ... ; and displaced into the nursery the vernacular discipline of an 'authorized' crib. Formal scholarship became an indispensable prerequisite to study of Mediterranean culture. ...

Sir John Myres

Perhaps if I had been introduced to the ancients through their history and customs, instead of through their grammar and syntax, I might have had a better [school] record.

Sir Winston Churchill

Introduction

Ancient Greece and Rome have held a fascination of one sort or another for people as diverse as Keats and Michael Ayrton, Racine and Giraudoux, Walter Savage Landor and Mary Renault, Offenbach and Stravinsky, Claude Lorraine and Henry Moore; and for the schoolboy who wrote in a mock GCE examination:

I was born on the day of the Salamais. That same day my father died at the hand of a Persian, and my mother refused to see me. So my nurse, following the Spartan tradition, left me alone in the hills to die. ...

The civilizations of Greece and Rome are a country of the mind, founded on reality. The reality is partly, but never more than partly,

6

recoverable. The country is inhabited not only by half the Great Men of History, but also by engaging minor notables such as: Solon, Themistocles, Cleon and Alcibiades; by the enterprising Clodius and his unconventional sister; by Catullus who did not care whether Caesar were white or black, and Horace who cared rather too much that Augustus should be white in the world's eyes; by Nero, Poppaea and Octavia — archetypes of vice and virtue; also by the nameless Athenians who died on the banks of the Assinarus, by Xenophon's comrades in arms and by the slaves who fought with Spartacus. The country has impressive sites — Mycenae, Delphi, the Acropolis and the Palatine — and fine buildings. It has delightful and fearful scenery — the vale of Tempe, the pass of Thermopylae, the meadows pastured by the flocks of Daphnis and Tityrus, the Ciminian forest, the bay of Baiae and the bloodstained oak grove of Mona. All these we can approach but never attain, not even if we become accomplished scholars. We can look on the ruins of the Parthenon or Hadrian's Wall, but only in the imagination can they be re-created. It is a country in which we can travel hopefully for the rest of our lives with no danger of ever arriving.

If pupils who take courses in Classical Studies do not feel something of this enchantment, then it will remain an academic subject for them, to be thankfully forgotten the moment they are released from school. However, to earn a place in a crowded timetable Classical Studies will be expected to do more than kindle an imaginative interest. It will be expected to foster skills and develop attitudes of mind. Antiquity can and should be a stimulus to thought as well as to imagination. This may pose a dilemma. How much importance is the teacher to place on historical truth, and how much should he encourage fantasy? How worried should he be by anachronisms; as when, in a spirited rendering of the return of Odysseus, zero hour for the massacre of the suitors is fixed by a wristwatch; or when a group of pupils, collaboratively writing a playlet about the building of a temple, make the construction work depend on slave labour more suited to the erection of a pyramid?

Theoretical considerations

An eminent educationist has proposed a law that no one should be allowed to campaign for the introduction of a new subject into the curriculum unless he is prepared to say what he would extrude to make way for it. Such an interdict need not apply to Classical Studies if it is seen as one end of a continuum, the other end being the *linguistic* gateway into the Ancient World, in other words Latin and Greek. Seen thus Classical Studies is no intruder. However, it is proposed to teach it to pupils who never learnt Latin. I am encouraged by colleagues whose concern is the teaching of English to believe that classical antiquity has

7

so much to offer towards the imaginative development of children that no enlightened English teacher would oppose its introduction into the curriculum even if it meant the loss of some periods formally labelled English; and many intelligent historians would feel much the same in relation to their own subject. The teaching of Latin, as we shall see, has inherited an excessive burden of justificatory theory; Classical Studies is still dangerously (if refreshingly) innocent in respect of its theory. There are currently a number of rather crude and dismal theories, which could lead to crude and dismal practice, such as: that the function of Classical Studies is to keep the Classics teacher in employment so that he can continue his proper task, which is the teaching of Latin and Greek to a select few; that its function is to be a bait to catch bright pupils for next year's Latin beginners' class; that in a proper selective school everyone should be capable of learning Latin, but now the Goths are at the gate, if not actually inside it, thought must be given to civilizing them. Too barbarous for Latin, they might nevertheless make something of Classical Studies, which thus becomes an inferior substitute for Latin.

The most interesting thinking about the function of Classical Studies can, perhaps, be rather arbitrarily grouped under two separate but not opposed headings.

Theory A

This theory believes that many of the categories of thought, much of the segmentation of reality and experience, many of the ways of viewing the world and man's activities in it (or however this idea is expressed) that are implicit in the thinking and behaviour of modern civilized man derive from our Graeco-Roman inheritance. Inasmuch as the function of education is initiation into society and its values and achievements, every pupil should be initiated into the Greek (or Roman) archetypes of our categories of thought. Against the objection that they are better encountered in their fully developed form, it can be argued that they are much more easily comprehended when seen in the less complicated context of Ancient Rome or Ancient Athens as we know them. To put it more simply: the language we use when discussing ethics and politics derives from the criticism by Plato and Aristotle of their own societies; our literary criticism from the observations of Aristotle and Horace on classical literary practice; our artistic canons are based on Renaissance study of antique art forms; our very assumptions about the nature of man are inherited as much from Greek as from Hebrew thought. All this is so embedded in our complex civilization that it is easier and more effective to teach the elements of, for example, political theory through the study of Athenian democracy

8

rather than through the study of modern political ideologies or organizations; and the elements of ethics through the career of Socrates rather than through a textbook of modern ethical theory.

Theory B

This theory begins from the eleven-year-old or twelve-year-old child and asks what the Ancient World can contribute to his intellectual, imaginative and social development. The answer is likely to make reference to the imaginative richness of Greek mythology and the freedom it gives to project fantasy unrestricted by the laws of nature: to the quality of Greek epic, which contains both the childlike and unreal, but psychologically significant, logic of the fairy-tale and the normative nobility of legend, as well as realistic observation of human character and motivation; to the 'Just-so story' quality of the invention of the alphabet, of ostracism, the Pnyx and the law courts, of early Greek science and Greek technology; and finally the theory may adduce the value of diminishing our uncritical ethnocentricity through the attempt to understand the values of a different civilization. Crudely the two theories may be categorized as (A) Education *in* Classics; (B) Education *through* Classics.

Though they are not incompatible, an exclusive adherence to either of the two theories could lead to *practices* that were incompatible: to a failure, in the one case, to engage pupils imaginatively in the material they study, so that it remains external information of no value to them personally; in the other case, to an imaginative approach which showed a cavalier incuriosity about the realities of the ancient world and no concern for authenticity. Theory A might appeal to the philosopher or the historian; Theory B to the psychologist or the English teacher.

Objectives

Statements of objectives are valuable to teachers as an aid to reflection about the success or failure of what they are doing, necessary to the constructors of syllabuses and examination papers, and useful as points of reference in discussion. However, the strict adherence of good teachers to theoretical objectives is happily frustrated by their responsiveness to the unpredictable needs and interests of their classes, and by the unruliness of their own enthusiasms. No one has yet propounded a definitive set of objectives for Classical Studies. Required once to outline a goal for a five-year course, I suggested that pupils should emerge from their learning capable of more or less informed discussion of the following (which I consider compatible with both Theory A and Theory B):

9

1 The essential differences between the democracy of fifth-century Athens and of modern Britain;
2 The essential differences between the religion (beliefs and practices) of fifth-century Athens and modern Christianity;
3 The sources of conflict between state and individual as illustrated by Sophocles' *Antigone* and the career of Socrates;
4 The significant differences between modern and ancient warfare and attitudes towards it;
5 The basic differences between the conventional attitudes of fifth-century Athenians and modern Englishmen towards death, destiny, progress, the unity of mankind, women and work;
6 The standards of living generally considered adequate for a cultured life in fifth-century Athens and modern Britain − with Augustan Rome and Victorian England thrown in for further comparison. (How much did the state provide and how important was it to have money or property?);
7 The main differences between educational ideas and practices in fifth-century Athens and modern Britain.

This list has been severely criticized both for being restrictive and for involving concepts too advanced to bear any relation to what can be done in years one and two. None the less, I continue to defend it − for want of a better set of objectives − on the grounds that all the activities that I consider desirable in years one and two would have the effect of helping the pupil to develop an imaginative understanding of Ancient Athens necessary to internalizing his subsequent knowledge of the social and political facts and to set them within his framework of judgments, beliefs and attitudes, in respect of politics and religion. If his course has done this for him it will have done more than an old-fashioned classical education did for some of its pupils, and, if at the end of five years it has done much less, then I think it must have dissipated its efforts very superficially. To the objection that nothing of Spartacus, Nero or the oak grove of Mona appears in my list I would answer that it is proper for a CSE/O-level course to converge on a time and place in which the interrelations of the cultural unity mentioned by Wilamowitz can be studied. Those pupils who continue to study the ancient world in the Sixth Form can then branch out into hitherto unexplored times and places.

Short-term objectives

Such a long-term objective would require short-term objectives to take account of those pupils who, so to speak, dropped off the Classical Studies train, or joined it at intermediate stations; as also for those who proposed to go on to further destinations at A-level or university. One thing, at least, is certain: that Classical Studies must be seen as a stop-ping train and not as an express; or, in more academic parlance, as a horizontal subject, not a vertical one. This is because of the precarious-ness of its place in the timetable in the foreseeable future, rather than because of its inherent nature; and, when we come to discuss organiza-tion, certain reservations will have to be made about its horizontality.

I shall not invite further criticism by proposing a list of short-term objectives, but merely suggest that such objectives should not be in-compatible with my five-year goal. Short-term objectives are likely to be heavily influenced by the circumstances in which the course takes place. Classical Studies at the 'Foundations Course' (i.e. eleven-year-old and twelve-year-old) level often exists by courtesy of the History, or Religious Education or (most likely) English departments. In any of these cases it is clearly incumbent on its teachers to attempt some of the objectives which these subjects would have aimed at. Such a con-sideration may modify the design of the course.

Let us consider at this point some of the things that teachers of English say about their work, both because it is their territory that Classical Studies may be encroaching on, and because they, unlike Classics teachers, have a long tradition of teaching pupils of all abilities; and because the sort of excellence they aim at is much more relevant to Classical Studies than the analytical abilities which are expected of the promising classicist. Also, theoretical discussion of English teaching is based on a body of international research into language and its function in the development of thought and personality which has, unlike much research into learning theory, been built into a coherent set of ideas comprehensible to teachers; and finally both Classical Studies and English use myth and story-telling.

Here is a distinguished teacher of English writing about his one-year course for a junior form in a secondary school:

[It] is not based on the notion that English teaching is centrally a matter of skills instruction, not even that it is centrally concerned with drawing pupils into an established cultural tradition. Both ele-ments are present, the linguistic and the cultural, and ideally the teacher will be conscious of both as ongoing traditions, but they could lay a dead hand on the pupil. If we once regard the pupil as a growing person with a living imagination, and accept that his use of language, involving the self and a direct response to experience, is essential to his growth, then the whole focus shifts for the teacher.

With this focus, the teacher looks centrally at the pupil's response to the situation, in class and out of it, and to the material presented by the teacher or offered by the pupils themselves. The teacher guides the response towards various activities such as talk, story-writing, poetry-making, drama, observation, collecting and classifying

11

facts and objects, and all the time he offers skills as needed, encourages improved performance, looks for individual excellence. Above all, as English teacher he looks for the individual and original utterances of language, whether written or spoken, by which each pupil makes experience his own, and he works on that. (John Watts, *Interplay One*)

A teacher specially interested in the contribution of Classics to general education is, perhaps characteristically, more specific. His aim is that all children should learn:

1 to comprehend and demonstrate comprehension of human situations presented in story form,
2 to tolerate and sympathize with characters and behaviour which may at this stage be outside their immediate experience,
3 to articulate opinions and emotions and to sustain sensible discussion,
4 to co-operate in the production of group assignments with children of different ability, temperament and background,
5 to adapt themselves to the available resources and to recognize their own strengths and weaknesses. (Stephen Sharp, in *Didaskalos* 4, 2 (1973))

The two statements are not strictly comparable. The one is mainly about methods, the other about aims; but they have this in common, that neither teacher is interested in the content of his course except for its capacity to contribute to developmental needs of the pupil. Not all teachers of Classical Studies will want to adopt this attitude (which derives almost exclusively from Theory B on p. 9): some may feel that it begs the question, 'Then, why teach about the *ancient* world?' To this Stephen Sharp might answer, 'Because it lends itself to my aims quite as well as the modern world, and I happen to have been educated as a classicist.'

A sociological digression

Much has been talked and written about the alienation of working-class pupils as the result of schools trying to engraft in them a middle-class culture. The argument is quite complex and embraces consideration of, *inter alia*, the allegedly different child-rearing habits of working-class families and the effect of these on attitudes to academic work and to career ambitions. In its cruder forms the argument implies that e.g. Shakespeare, Mozart, Ancient Greece, consideration for others, respect for communal property and speech free from Nixonian expletives are appropriate only for those born into the middle classes; and that schools should not interfere with the birthright of the working-class boy, which is pop entertainment, club football, the 750 cc motor bicycle, beer and bingo. It would be foolish to disparage these amenities: even vandalism and obscenity may have a function when one has a grudge against the world (and which of us has not at some time or other enjoyed the licensed vandalism of the Aunt Sally stall?). Cultural priggishness is a short cut to the alienation of pupils and the teacher of Classical Studies will need to take account of the material environment and home culture of his pupils. However, if it is permissible for a non-sociologist to express an opinion based on non-scientific observation and in non-sociological language, I would hazard the following (which begs discussion of the terms 'working-class' and 'middle-class' and the sub-subcultures those terms comprehend): in so far as there *are* opposing tendencies, being middle-class includes a willingness to affect tastes and interests that are not genuine (but may become so) in order to better oneself socially, intellectually or materially; whereas being working-class inclines one towards a self-conscious hostility to tastes and interests that are unfamiliar and could therefore be judged affected. However, the philistinism that results from this latter tendency is no more aggressive and intractable than the philistinism of the old-fashioned public-school boy, who was similarly fixated in conformism to the attitudes of his age-group. As the word *Classics* loses its Oxbridge and upper-class connotations, Classical Studies will suffer from such philistinism as much as any other non-utilitarian subject — and no more. The eleven-year-old pupil who had this to say about Theseus and the Minotaur:

I don't care whether that monster ate him or not. I don't need any of this. I'm going to be a bus conductor . . .

could have taken an equally jaundiced view of any History, Religious Education, or English lesson which did not appear to be teaching him useful skills. As we have seen from the words of John Watts, language is regarded by an English teacher as having a far more important, subtle and pervasive function in education than could be discharged in the mere acquisition of standard spelling, punctuation and syntax, and BBC elocution. Classical Studies can do more for pupils than impart an unwanted ability to participate in upper-class cultural chit-chat (though one of its objectives could be to facilitate enjoyment of literature created when study of Greek and Roman authors was synonymous with education).

Cultural stratification is to be combated, not condoned. 'Born a man, died a grocer' should be no man's epitaph. No one should die a grocer, or bus conductor, or company director, or schoolmaster or university lecturer. This is not to say that the teacher of Classical Studies should not beware of translating the ancient world into an exclusively middle-class idiom. The warning applies not only to stuffy language but to a presentation that glosses over slavery, infanticide, exploitation of the lower classes, the violence and cruelty of political life in Greece and Rome, and the ruthlessness of ancient imperialism. The dangers of this sort of treatment are much diminished since we have ceased to see the Greeks and Romans as 'Fellows of another College', fit to grace High Table or the Liberal benches of the House of Commons. Admittedly, the major characters of Ancient History cannot, without distortion, be presented as other than members of the middle or, more likely, upper classes, with all that may imply in the context of their times, but the exploration of their personalities is a sophisticated undertaking which must anyhow await a maturity which will have, one may hope, dissolved the obstructions raised by crude class-consciousness.

The early stages

The most widely favoured method of presentation in the early stages, and the one that seems best adapted to the wide range of abilities to be found in most Classical Studies classes in the first year, is that known as 'the story-centred approach', which leads on to a varied range of activities. Narrative is the manner in which societies in an early stage of cultural development organize their beliefs, rules and knowledge of the past (myth and legend); it is also the form in which adolescents at an early stage of mental development find knowledge most easy to assimilate. Writing as one who, in middle age, is still addicted to narrative for this purpose, I feel confident that it has an important part to play at all levels of Classical Studies. However, at Foundations Course level the 'story-centred approach' and its follow-up activities can be made to sound quite dismal.

Teacher tells one of the hackneyed stories — say Theseus and the Minotaur — known already to half the children from their primary school days, then asks them a few questions to make sure they have been listening; after that he tells them to disperse into groups and paint the Minotaur, or write a playlet about the elopement of Theseus and Ariadne, or make a plasticine model of the labyrinth, or a tape-recorded account of an afternoon in the bull-ring, or write the front-page of the 'Minoan Times' for the day after the earthquake — and stay out of trouble until the end of the double lesson. There ensue forty-five minutes of desultory activity, interspersed with hastily suppressed scuffles, lengthy gossip about boy-friends or pop idols, and a total lack of engagement with the story that began the lesson.

Nothing could better raise the hackles of the traditionalist Classics teacher, habituated to teaching a 'vertical' subject which gave him copious opportunities for assessing progress and conveying a sense of achievement. He will be tempted to prefer a method in which the ancient world is presented *ex cathedra*, parcelled up into small items of knowledge to be copied into notebooks and regurgitated on demand — a crude interpretation of Theory A (p. 8). But our dismal account of the story-centred approach describes merely what can happen when it is used by a teacher who does not really believe in the theories of learning and development which underlie it. All the activities mentioned can be carried out in a manner and a spirit likely to develop useful skills as well as foster the assimilation of the ideas and knowledge that the pupils have derived from the story. Very much hinges on the quality of the story-telling and of the questioning and discussion that follow from it (the object of which is to provoke reflection on its moral and psychological implications, and on its relation to the pupils' own lives), and then on the skill and sensitivity of the teacher in fostering the individual pupil's response. Of course his task is made infinitely easier or more difficult by the predisposition of the pupils to be interested and enterprising or apathetic and disruptive — and this may largely depend on their experiences in primary school. In the first case his problem will be to offer a sufficiently varied scope for lively imaginations, in the second to provide a strong organization of activities, and the discipline of a recognized routine to follow a resourceful and flexible variety of stimuli. (The stimulus need not always be a story, and much may be learnt from good English courses which interweave visual and non-verbal sound stimuli with the verbal stimuli of poetry and prose.)

The story — myth and legend

Myths, legends and fairy stories from many cultures are a feature of English lessons in the primary school, where they have found their way from the Victorian nursery, together with children's rhymes, songs and games. They are now there by right of educational theory. Does the presentation of specifically Greek myths and legends as the staple of Classical Studies Foundations Courses imply that these courses are merely 'English' under another name, or is the use to be made of them subtly different? First a few observations on the nature of myths and legends, and on their possible function in the psychological development of children.

Myths and legends are not, as has been sometimes supposed, the naive creations of the primitive childhood of a people which discards them as it becomes civilized and sophisticated, so that one can simply say to pupils, 'These are charming but childish tales which illustrate the Greeks' love of a good story.' 'But did they believe such silly stuff?' 'Only the simple country folk, I expect.' For a start many of the stories are far from charming and, second, myth, religious and political, is always with us, whether we are fifth-century Greeks, first-century Romans or twentieth-century Englishmen. Despite the fact that History as a discipline is enshrined in our universities, the lay Englishman remains normally unaware how pervasive myth is in his own life. For most of us Cromwell, Wellington and Churchill are mythical entities, as are Merrie England, the Battle of the Boyne, the Industrial Revolution, the evacuation from Dunkirk and the heroism of the Blitz. We regard them as irreducible facts, just as our grandparents, or greatgrandparents, regarded as irreducible facts the Garden of Eden, Moses and the Ten Commandments, the Nativity of Christ, and St George and the Dragon. They are, of course, not facts but narratives. Even Churchill, as each of us knows him, is in a sense a narrative, governed by our predisposition to see him as a national hero, a bellicose imperialist or an enemy of the woiking classes.

The purpose of this second digression is to suggest that myth and history are at opposite ends of a continuum. The extent to which a narrative is myth is a measure of the extent that the social, religious, psychological or emotional needs of a society or of an individual have been projected into it, and the extent to which it is history is a measure of the extent to which it is the product of disciplined enquiry, using all the available tools of investigation devised by historians since the science was invented by the Greeks for attempting to uncover and represent the truth about the past. By this definition, of course, a very great deal of Greek and Roman history is at the mythical end of the continuum and will remain there despite some successes of modern historians and archaeologists in shifting it a little way towards the other end. If myth is still influential in our lives today, when our education is mainly secular, scientific and rational, it must have been many times more so in the Ancient World; so an acquaintance with Greek and Roman myths can be an important first step towards an understanding of their societies. This answers the query whether the 'story-centred approach' in Classical Studies is merely 'English' under another name: but there is always the danger that in seeking to be something more than 'merely English', it may, by inhibiting imagination in the cause of authenticity, end up by being much less than English. A myth is subtly, or crudely, different each time it is retold — whether by a Greek mother to her child, by Sophocles to the audience at the Greater Dionysia, by Anouilh, by Seraillier or by the Classical Studies teacher himself; and when the myth is told orally by a story-teller sensitive to his audience, they too will participate in the creation of a new version. A story-teller so gifted that he can (and does) go into classrooms where he is unknown and hold the children spellbound, says that while telling his story he *believes* every word of it — he must be Oedipus and experience the terrifying shifts of emotion of that amazing man, before he can tell his story properly. For him and for his audience it is a living experience of alarming and absorbing truth.

The developmental functions of myth

The analytical psychologists (Jungians) have powerful theories about the significance of myth for the adolescent, and the assistance it provides in emancipating him from the strong and inhibiting emotional ties of childhood. Though persuasive, they are not proven and may not convince many teachers. None the less, it is not difficult to recognize that adolescence is a period when the imaginary terrors of childhood are not yet quite outgrown and are joined by fears of humiliation and rejection, crises of identity, conflict between continued need for the security of home and the desire for independence, the pains of first love and ambivalent feelings about sex. Without any prompting from adults, adolescents will find their own mythical figures in sporting or pop idols; and these have a useful role, not least in helping the adolescent to develop feelings of solidarity with his peers; but the experiences encountered by adolescents are too rich, subtle and complex to be adequately catered for by these myths alone. Other vehicles are needed for the projection of the inner world of hopes, fears, loves and hates which these experiences create. Such a vehicle is provided for the older adolescent by novels, films and television drama: for the younger adolescent it can be provided for by myths as well as by children's stories.

The question is sometimes asked: if listening to (or reading) a story of myth or fiction is *intrinsically* helpful to the psychological development of a young adolescent, why the superaddition of all the follow-up activities? It is well that the question should be asked, for there is a danger that the myth may be regarded as no more than a peg on which to hang activities designed to foster particular skills. After all, parents who read fairy stories to their children at bedtime do not afterwards expect them to model a witch in plasticine, or write a poem about dragons. Surely there must be a case for occasionally telling the myth at the *end* of the lesson, and letting the pupils make of it what they can and will on their own. None the less there are good reasons for saying that the myth can do more for the pupils when they are encouraged to recreate it for themselves.

The story — history

It can safely be said that History, in the academic sense, cannot be

practised in the lower forms of the secondary school. This is not because of a lack of time-sense. The oft-quoted inability of certain ten-
year-olds, despite a term spent studying social life under the Stuarts, to
dissociate mud huts and human sacrifice from the reign of Charles I,
could simply be the result of the manner in which information had
been presented to them. Would they have made the same mistakes, one
wonders, if they had heard Geoffrey Trease's *The Grey Adventurer* read
to them? The real problem is twofold. First, the doings of mankind that
occupy the pages of most history text-books spring from motivations·
and calculations that are too far removed from the experience of ten-
year-olds to be comprehensible to them. Second, a critical understanding of the many limitations on any historian's ability to recreate the
past is beyond the grasp of a ten-year-old, so that to him (and, for that
matter, to most fourteen-year-olds) History is simply what is written
in a history text-book.

This is not to say that no history can be sensibly undertaken by
pupils in the lower forms of secondary school. Local history, and the
history of early technology, for example, need present neither of the
difficulties mentioned. Much of Ancient History, as has already been
observed, is nine-tenths legend, and therefore lends itself to elementary
exercises in the useful habit of asking, 'Did it really happen?'

The treatment of legend for this purpose will clearly have to differ
sharply from the treatment of legend (and myth) for the purpose of
stimulating children's fantasy. The specifically *historical* follow-up to
Agamemnon and Mycenae, Theseus and Crete, Leonidas and Thermopylae is obviously not going to be an imaginative exercise such as 'Write
a story in which you are a commander with the choice between facing
certain destruction in a fight against immense odds, and saving yourself
and your men by retreat' (not that such an exercise might not have
value for a future historian), but a study of Schliemann and Evans, their
methods, their mistakes and how much and how little they have
proved, of bronze-age weapons, armour and fortifications, of the geography of Central Greece and the tactics of the Greek hoplite. One of
the advantages of Classical Studies is that it offers such an open choice
in planning the early course. My own inclination would be to combine,
or rather alternate, the imaginative and the historical treatment, in
preference to offering a year of undiluted fantasy. Nor need all the
historical treatment originate in the telling of a story. If the teacher
has any skill as a technologist, some investigation into the technology
of the trireme, of the Greek Stage and its machinery, into the tensile
strength and range of a Persian bow or a Roman catapult, or into
the techniques of temple construction — all these might make a wel-
come diversion from myth.

Talk

Group activity, rather than individual study, is frequently recommended to the teacher of Classical Studies. The justification often given is that it is important for pupils to learn to collaborate. So it is, but there is another theoretically good reason for group activity, and that is the opportunities it offers for talk. The theory presupposes an adequate degree of motivation among the pupils, enough for them to want to get on with their collaborative tasks, and not simply to gossip. Tape recordings made of groups of children engaged on solving some problem together seem to indicate that the exercise of pooling their resources of knowledge and understanding can lead to the conversion of what was mere academic information into knowledge that can be related to the sum of the pupil's previous knowledge, and utilized in argument, reflection and speculation. I imagine that many classical graduates would benefit their scholarship if they sat down in groups of five to collaborate in the writing of a historical novel set in, say, Periclean Athens or the Rome of Augustus. The exercise of getting the hero out of his house, down the street to the city centre and into conversation with his associates on politics, religion, philosophy, or merely talking city gossip — this would reveal gaps in knowledge and understanding that would be self-evident or if not, soon spotted and plugged by other members of the group, or would exact recourse to a dictionary of antiquities. The critical standards of a group of eleven-year-olds would be less vigilant, and might even produce the equivalent of mud huts and idol-worship in Stuart England; but if the conversation were tape-recorded for the teacher, he could show the pupils how to correct their misconceptions by reference to text or pictures. Had the follow-up to the teacher's exposition been an essay or note-taking, the misconceptions could well have gone unrevealed. However, it is when the follow-up is to be an imaginative exercise, involving moral issues and drawing on the pupils' own experience of life, that most value is claimed for talk. Again tape recordings have shown that the social enjoyment of exchanging experiences has led to the articulation of feelings, impressions and judgments to a degree most unlikely in a class discussion led by a teacher. Not that the unobtrusive presence and occasional tactful intervention of the teacher may not help a group discussion along.

Writing

Investigations conducted on behalf of the Schools Council have revealed that a very high proportion of the writing done by pupils in school can be categorized as writing addressed to the teacher in his role of examiner, and written as though its function were to convey information. (In fact, of course, the teacher knows it all already, so that the real function is to enable the teacher to mark, assess, grade or criticize the pupil's learning performance.) Informational writing is, of course, highly important in adult life, and written work provides, in many subjects, by far the most effective means for the teacher to gauge his own success or failure as well as the diligence and ability of his pupils. Nevertheless, writing has many other social uses, and Classical Studies will provide opportunities for the written work to be directed towards other pupils; towards the outside community; towards the writer himself; and towards the teacher seen in other roles than as examiner — and to have other functions than conveying information, e.g. to crystallize speculative or reflective thought, and to carry the language which children (and adults too) use, often obliquely, for accommodating themselves to the shocks and sufferings to which they are exposed. All these types of writing should help the pupil to make the knowledge he acquires in his Classical Studies lessons his own, something he does not gladly abandon the moment he is released from school. It was suggested earlier that the ultimate goal for a five-year course was that the pupils should be capable of informed *discussion* of various aspects of the Ancient World. This presupposes the habit of handling their knowledge, seeing it from various angles, and believing in it as something of significance. It was once observed and documented that pupils well grounded in biology, physics and chemistry, and possessed of the 'lines of evidence' for the theory of evolution, were still unable to argue coherently against an anti-Darwinian: the solution found to this problem of inert knowledge was to organize discussion between fellow-students so as to focus attention not only on scientific conclusions, but also on the way in which the conclusions were reached.

An alternative to the story-centred approach

A possible alternative method of teaching Classical Studies, which I know to have been considered by several teachers, but which I have not yet seen tried, is through language. The only suitable course for such a method would be the Cambridge Latin Course, which could be described as an elementary course in the sociology of the ancient world, consisting as it does of well-researched story material in Latin, supported by 'paralinguistic' chapters in English, dealing with sociological and archaeological information about life in the first century AD. If the teacher were free from any concern to teach skill in the language, so that he could move as slowly or as fast through the course as he wished, concerned only that the pupils should be able to follow the stories, while concentrating on the sociological and archaeological elements, he would have a focus of interest in the fortunes of the skilfully drawn characters of the story, and could use the language as a quarry for the discussion of cultural differences between the Roman world and our own. However, all this is speculation.

Additional stimuli

A teacher who was not too afraid of the temporal confusions alleged by some experts to be rife among ten- and eleven-year-olds, might try interspersing his Greek myths with mediaeval fairy tales and Arthurian legends. It has been observed that the view of life presented by myths and folk-tales differs across cultures far less than the 'furniture' with which they operate. The cylindrical turrets of the Gothic castle appear above the oaks or pines of a heavily forested mountain while the squat and massive Mycenaean citadel is perched on bare rock; the Greek hero, chariots notwithstanding, travels and fights on foot, the mediaeval hero on horseback. Trolls, ogres, Cyclopes and djinns are much the same under the skin; but are there not significant differences between Odysseus and Sinbad, Jason and Sir Percival, Medea and Morgan le Fay, Siegfried and Achilles — significant enough to make comparisons interesting?

Few teachers nowadays are so placed that they cannot incorporate museum-visiting into their programmes. The profit that pupils get from this visiting very much depends on what they bring to it. An object seen in a museum is not unlike a stranded whale: it gives the onlooker a very inadequate idea of its nature and function in its original environment. The imaginative effort to envisage this environment must depend largely on what scheme of associations the pupil has acquired before his visit — though good museums now try to float their whales in a skilful simulation of their natural habitat. Another task in museum-visiting is to teach children to *look at* objects, not just to read the labels: and for some teachers the first stage in the task is to teach *themselves* to do this. Some museums and some teachers issue the visiting pupils with questionnaires to concentrate their activities and attention on certain objects and certain aspects of those objects; but too often the questions asked are to be answered by simply reading the label attached to the objects. Careful thought is needed to frame questions which require the pupils to look hard at an object and ask themselves what it can tell them about its function, construction and efficiency; and about the purposes of the artist who made it; and about the methods, skill and success with which these purposes have been achieved.

No one would wish to re-establish the brief fashion for illustrating Latin course books with G. F. Watts's sentimental minotaur, the Aldobrandini Marriage and Alma-Tadema's languorous banquets and slave-markets: but in Classical Studies there should be a place for slides of Picasso's minotaurs, Minoan frescoes, ancient jewellery and armour, as well as of Greek sites and landscapes. A very selective use of excerpts from modern novels set in the ancient world is another resource, and a musically knowledgeable teacher might do much with operatic interpretations of Greek myths.

The organization of a five-year course

It has been already remarked that a Classical Studies course must be organized on a year-to-year basis. However, where some of the pupils who begin at eleven may continue until O-level or CSE – or even further – it is worth considering whether there is any logical progression. If there is, it will be based on a consideration of the concepts which will have to be mastered by the final year. If we accept the goals suggested on page 10 then some mastery of Athenian political, religious and educational thought and practice will be demanded. These are complex and difficult subjects, and the bane of History, Sociology and Religion, as school subjects, is the persistence of unassimilated abstractions and concepts – counters which can be manipulated to provide some sort of answer to an essay question, but which are not currency that the pupil can use in any other context (like the trained Darwinians mentioned earlier). The concept of Athenian democracy could perhaps be built up steadily by discovering the topography of Ancient Athens, with its places of assembly (formal and informal) which made it a 'face-to-face' society; by encountering the jury system in action in *The Wasps*; by reading of the Battle of Arginusae, its aftermath and the conduct of Socrates as President of the Council; by learning of Sparta's military education and social organization by way of contrast. Similarly, understanding of Athenian religion should be underpinned by knowledge about Greek temples and their construction, the rituals connected with them, the myths and the priesthood, Delphi and Eleusis – in brief, by building up the concept from familiarity with the concrete elements of which the abstraction is a synthesis, and by seeing these elements functioning in plausible situations – which is where Aristophanic comedy is so valuable, if used critically, and also, if used critically, historical novels such as those by Treece, Seraillier, Rosemary Sutcliffe or Mary Renault.

Classical Studies as part of a Humanities Course

In many schools the title 'Humanities' has been annexed (without intended disrespect to Cicero, Renaissance educators or Scottish Departments of Latin) by courses in a combination of any or all of the following: History, Ancient History, Art History, English, Geography and Religious Knowledge. A distinction is sometimes made between 'integrated' Humanities and 'inter-related' Humanities. If integrated, the course is expected to be planned under such a title (sometimes referred to as a 'supra-concept') as 'Shelter' or 'Transport' or 'Festivals', and a common programme is taught, with only slight individual variations, by all the members of the team. If the course is inter-related, then each member teaches his own programme, with a bias towards his own subject specialism, but all the programmes have a common theme and the pupil-groups move from one teacher to another at fixed intervals.

If the course is integrated and the dominant member of the team is a geographer, then it is liable to be made up of volcanoes, the planetary system, glaciation, fossils, continental drift, the dinosaurs and other topics not obviously humane. (This does not imply any belittlement of geographers, whose subject is fascinating and undervalued, and whose contribution to a Humanities course is all but essential. It is merely a consequence of their present enthusiasm for 'earth science' and the glories of the Geological Museum in South Kensington.)

If the course is inter-related and a historian is in charge then there is a fair chance that a classicist will be able to contribute more than a mere excursus on mythology to explain the names of the planets, together with a brief run-down on Pompeii, Thera and Atlantis as his contribution to vulcanology.

The Cave of Trophonius (more generally known as Objective Educational Research) is beginning to give responses more pleasing to conservatives than to progressives. Most oracles, whatever their record of veracity, are sensitive to the Zeitgeist, so we can perhaps expect educational opinion to favour the new styles of teaching less than in recent decades. None the less, classicists would be unwise to feel they can now dismiss, with a sigh of relief, all thought of Team-teaching and Humanities courses. New wine is still likely to be needed for new bottles, and inter-related teaching is logically sound and quite practicable, at least in the early years of secondary schooling when pupils cannot all be expected to take at once to specialist teaching on leaving their primary schools. Most topics that a classicist is likely to be interested in can be better understood if taught with reference to environmental factors, and only the arrogant or obtuse will not gain something from working alongside his colleagues from the Art, RE, History and English Departments. It does no harm to consider from time to time the nature of the divisions of knowledge (or of 'reality') into subject specialisms. Presumably 'History', 'Geography' and 'Religion' were simultaneously present in the consciousness of the Athenians who fought in Sicily, of the craftsmen who worked on the temple of Zeus at Olympia, of the Spaniards who guarded Hadrian's Wall and of the Roman officials who governed Egypt: does it make sense to separate them for the purpose of teaching Ancient — or, for that matter, Mediaeval or Modern — History?

It is not any logical weakness that threatens the future of inter-subject teaching, but human frailty — the lack of those virtues of Modesty, Sympathy and Tolerance required by teachers who work together on a Humanities team. Add to these virtues Industriousness, the capacity for constructive planning and the willingness to subject your performance to the critical eyes of your colleagues and it may be felt that the demands of Team-teaching are beyond what one can reasonably expect from any individual in a pagan society.

It is a good fashion which labels difficulties a Challenge, instead of treating them as the signal for retreat. This, then, is the basic difficulty of an inter-subject Humanities course: the pupils — some, if not all of them — will later be taking public exams in History, English, Geography and, perhaps, Religious Education. On the one hand the historians, English teachers, geographers and Religious Educationists of the team must show a chivalrous respect for the distinctive knowledge and skills of their colleagues, and, on the other hand, they must insist that the skills and knowledge that are basic to their own courses get adequate teaching. Careful planning, frequent meetings, tactful and intelligent leadership and friendly relations are all essential.

Where then does the classicist come in? Perhaps he has to exercise the greatest tolerance of all, having to learn strange periods of history and new skills in order to earn a pitch for Greek and Roman antiquity and the right to see that these are taught properly. Axiomatic to Humanities is the maxim that the more deeply a teacher knows and cares about a period or topic, the better he will be able to extract the significant elements that can be taught to twelve-year-olds, and the significant details that will illuminate those elements. The converse, unfortunately, is even more true — superficiality of knowledge in the teacher can turn a course on Ancient Greece or anything else into a hotch-potch of trivialities and misinformation.

On worksheets

There are many good reasons for using worksheets in teaching Classical Studies or other like subjects. For one thing, there is seldom an ideal text-book for the needs of the course. Even streamed classes contain pupils with a wide diversity of talents and work styles. In a mixed-ability class some diversified organization of work is inevitable, unless the teacher expects to pitch his lesson at the level of his hypothetical average pupil and dragoon or cajole the rest into enduring boredom or bafflement.

In essence there is nothing new for a Classics teacher in worksheets. The traditional North and Hillard exercise is, in a sense, a worksheet.

It directs the activities of the pupils, and leaves to the teacher the role of supervisor, consultant and validator. Only the virtuoso teacher (a James Burke of the classroom) can engage the attention and interest of a large class for forty minutes four times a week. (Many otherwise progressive teachers have felt a twinge of regret for the days when they could say to their pupils, 'Get on with Exercise 41B and don't let me hear a murmur until you have finished sentences 5, 6, 8, 10 and 11.')

The teacher of Humanities is relieved by his worksheets from the need to be an ever-gushing fount of information and inspiration. It is a cliché that worksheets change the emphasis of the lesson from teaching to learning. Perhaps it would be more precise to say that the use of worksheets changes the classroom activity from what the teacher assumes is teaching to what he hopes is learning. Whether what takes place really is learning depends on the skill with which the worksheets have been composed.

On writing worksheets

This is a highly skilled and time-consuming task. It is nearly as demanding as writing a text-book, but more rewarding — except financially — because the writer can see his handiwork in operation, note his mistakes for future rectification and take pleasure in his successes. The first stage is wide reading and the search for illustrative material — visual and aural as well as literary (anecdotal and documentary). Then comes the most difficult stage, that of selection and rejection. Finally the enjoyable stage: devising the tasks and questions. These should allow some choice of activity, and range from listening to a tape and recording some response (a necessary part of the course if the class contains non-readers) to 'research' in the library (or just reading certain specified pages in a book from the classroom book-box). It might include collaboratively writing and acting a classroom playlet (or taping a 'radio play') from a given scenario; drawing; painting; modelling; calculating distances; deciphering manuscripts; or describing details in a picture.

Such activities can, of course, be improvised from lesson to lesson, but the advantage of directing them through a worksheet is that they are then planned in tranquillity and with an eye to continuous development — something that only a master strategist could improvise from lesson to lesson. Besides, pupils trained in the use of worksheets can be left to organize much of their own work (under competent supervision) so that the absence of the regular teacher (briefly from the classroom, or for some days through illness) is far less disruptive of progress than it would otherwise be.

Ideally, teachers should be given a term's leave to write a set of worksheets for a year's course. In reality it has to be done in the holidays

25

and at week-ends — or else the worksheets may be bought ready-made
from certain publishers: a much less satisfying procedure.

Chapter three

On teaching the classical languages

The close analytical study of a compound Latin sentence affords a mental exercise analogous to and in some respects superior to that afforded by a mathematical problem; and it is, perhaps, not too much to say, that the thorough comprehension of the dependence and subdependence of clauses in such a sentence is incompatible with confusion of thought and obscurity of expression.

A writer in the *Journal of Education*, 1881

When it comes to linguistic form, Plato walks with the Macedonian swine-herd, and Confucius with the head-hunting savage of Assam.

E. Sapir, *Language*, 1921

Omnis lingua usu potius discitur quam praeceptis.

Johann Amos Comenius, *Ianua Linguarum*, 1631

General

There was a time, in the not so distant past, when the learning of Classical Greek, and more particularly of Classical Latin, was seen as an end in itself, entirely justifiable even for pupils who achieved no more than an ability to answer a small range of questions in accidence and syntax, construe texts from a limited number of Latin authors and turn simple English into grammatically correct Latin; and this as the goal of many years of study. As the length and intensity of study diminished to make room for other subjects, the range of questions became smaller, the simple English was reduced to a very limited number of sentence patterns, and the texts had to be selected from a shrinking number of authors, and then purged of linguistic difficulties.

To the question 'why was Latin taught?' there was both a historical and a pedagogical answer. The historical answer was that in the Middle

27

Ages and at the Renaissance it was the key to the superior wisdom of the Ancient World and to the piety of the Christian Fathers, as well as being the international language of Religion, Law, Politics, Scholarship, and so on. By the end of the eighteenth century there were only a few pedants who still considered the ancient wisdom superior, and the value of Latin for communication had become minimal. None the less, the force of educational inertia, and the association of classical learning with upper-class cultivation, ensured that Latin and Greek were still the staple of secondary education everywhere except in the institutions of unorthodoxy — the Dissenting Academies. When the education provided by the endowed schools came under attack from political radicals at the beginning of the nineteenth century, the vast majority of teachers were educated to teach nothing but Latin and Greek, and most secondary schools were organized — and endowed — to teach virtually nothing else either. However, inertia was not a widespread characteristic of the Victorian era, and many energetic teachers set out to reform the content and methods of the Classics they continued to teach. But they were on the defensive. It was no longer self-evident that Latin and Greek should bulk large in the curriculum; justifications were called for. The cultural value of the Greek and Latin literatures could be adduced for pupils who achieved a high proficiency in the languages (though at least one powerful critic denied that, *as studied*, the ancient authors could yield any cultural benefits to anyone); for the majority of indifferently successful pupils the value (as an intellectual training) of manipulating English into Latin and Latin into English, and of Latin syntax and accidence, analytically studied, was put forward as a cast-iron justification on the grounds adduced by the writer in the *Journal of Education* quoted at the head of this chapter. The modern subject of linguistics being then in its infancy, and largely confined to the study of Indo-European languages, it was possible for classical educators to claim that Latin and Greek represented a 'purer' state of language, while German, French and English, having lost some or most of their inflections, represented a state of degeneracy ('with a grammar less philosophical and perfect than that of the ancient languages', in the words of one writer).

Perhaps the value of exercising the mind on elementary Latin has sometimes been dismissed too readily. I have heard a distinguished professor of Sociology, whose first training was in Classics, argue that North and Hillard Latin exercises are the finest possible propaedeutic to Sociology, because they are eminently boring and because they teach an exact attention to language — high toleration of boredom and trained attention to language being more valuable ingredients of a good sociologist than starry-eyed enthusiasm for changing the world. Distinguished professors of Sociology have such *mana* that one cannot afford not to listen to them, but, unless all professors of Sociology are prepared to make proficiency in Latin composition a condition of entry to their over-populated courses, the recommendation of Latin for its superior power to induce boredom would be, now of all times, a short cut to extinction.

Boredom apart, it is still possible to find teachers who are convinced that elementary Latin grammar, sentence-composition and unseen work are important as a training in precision and accuracy, valuable in any walk of life. Unfortunately for them, in the eyes of the rest of the educational world the carpet was pulled from under their feet once and for all when experimental psychology appeared to establish that transfer of training arguments were untenable. In fact, subsequent psychological pronouncements have seemed to waver somewhat on transfer; nevertheless, the claims of Classics teachers leave unimpressed many of those who have experience of elementary Latin teaching, because inspection of candidates' O-level examination papers, if not observation in the classroom, quickly reveals that the experience of a very large proportion of Latin pupils was that of *failing* (because of lack of time, or of ability, or of good teaching, or of sufficient motivation, or of a combination of all or any of these) to learn precision and accuracy in the handling of elementary Latin sentences and unseens. What they did learn was a discouraging familiarity with red ink. (This observable fact does not, of course, disprove the theory that accuracy *can* be so taught. It is interesting to learn of certain Pakistani and Indian immigrant children who *ask* to be taught Latin in their free time, because, as taught to them, it is simple and logical and reassuringly free from ambiguities, unlike their English lessons which they find confusing.) As for the more 'philosophical' grammar of the ancient as opposed to the modern languages, this thinking has been scotched by the Comparative Linguists. Just as Anthropology has created a copernican revolution by extruding European civilization from the centre of the cultural universe (now a void), so Comparative Linguistics has extruded the Indo-European languages from the centre of the linguistic universe, and pronounced that, as far as accidence and syntax goes, languages do not reflect the cultural environment of their speakers — hence the observation from Sapir's *Language*, quoted at the head of this chapter. Now it is at his peril that anyone dares to claim any superiority for a fusional (*alias* inflectional) language over mainly isolating and agglutinative languages like English, or any special educational value for Greek and Latin *as languages* by comparison with Swahili or Sundanese.

If *pure* linguistics has undermined some of the traditional arguments for Latin, *applied* linguistics has made the traditional methods of teaching it look a little obsolete — going back as many of them do to the third century BC, or to Priscian, or Alcuin — and rather less up-to-date than the sixteenth-century practice of Ascham or the seventeenth-century *Ianua Linguarum* of Comenius. Applied linguistics is something of a mushroom, sprouting from the crash programmes devised by American academic linguists in the Second World War to train American servicemen — in a hurry — to speak a wide variety of languages, including several which had never been formally taught before. After the war it was thought by some that the radically new thinking about how to teach a language would be reflected in radically new and strikingly successful teaching programmes throughout the schools of the world. Thirty years later it cannot be said with confidence that this pentecostal event has yet taken place. There has been a great output of books on linguistic theory, a new discipline called Psycholinguistics, the creation of many new courses and the building of many language laboratories. The general effectiveness of language teaching may have been increased, but for most pupils the learning of a foreign language is still a slow and difficult accomplishment. The theories of the scholars have proved to be provisional, and not all of the scholars believe that their theories are applicable to teaching problems. Should we then listen to the conservatives and go back to North and Hillard?

Some historical considerations

The Ancient World contributed much to the theory of education, but at the level of elementary instruction the record is not impressive. There were no Pestalozzis or Froebels, or if there were they made no general impact. If we may judge from the literary sources and the papyrological discoveries, most teachers in the Ancient World were unimaginative and mean-spirited, and began that association between the teaching of Latin (or Greek) and flogging that has dogged classical education down the centuries. In linguistics the contributions of Plato, Aristotle, the Stoics and Dionysius Thrax are considerable; though outclassed, so the historians of linguistics tell us, by those of the Hindu grammarian Pānini. But there were no applied linguists. The teachers were teaching prescriptive rules for the literary registers of the language to pupils who could already speak in the colloquial register. The first teachers whom we know to have tackled the task of teaching Latin to non-Latin-speakers were Bede and Alcuin. They relied for their analysis of Latin on the Latin grammarians who had re-applied to their own language the categories devised by the Greeks; and because copying was then at a low ebb, so that one book for the teacher was likely to be the allocation per class, their course books took the form of dialogues about Latin grammar to be memorized by the pupils.

About AD 1000 Aelfric of Eynsham wrote a grammar of Latin in Anglo-Saxon for teaching purposes, a simplified version of the works of the late Latin grammarians Priscian and Donatus. It contained a significant new element; the claim that it would serve as an introduction to

Anglo-Saxon grammar; and thus began the use of Latin grammar as a Procrustean bed which other languages had to be made to fit. Hence the quarrel which general linguists and teachers of English have with Latin teachers who claim to be teaching English grammar. Grammatical categories, they object, are valid only for the language from whose study they are derived, and should not be imposed on other languages. Latin and Greek were sufficiently similar for Latin to be amenable to the categories of Greek grammar, but Anglo-Saxon has, formally speaking, only four noun cases to Latin's six, and no passive conjugation at all; while English has nothing of either, except a genitive. So far from a knowledge of Latin grammar being transferable to the understanding of English, it only causes false assumptions and confusion.

The scholastic age produced its Latin primer in Alexander de Villedieu's *Doctrinale*, which taught, in inelegant Latin verse, the rules of *contemporary* Latin, much influenced by the logic of the schools, and dispensed with the appeals to the authority of the Latin authors of the golden age which had been the basis of the grammars of Donatus and Priscian. Naturally the humanists, with their contempt for the scholastics, and their desire to recreate in their speech and correspondence the elegance of Cicero, threw out the *Doctrinale* and replaced it with their own grammars and elementary colloquies (in England, Lily's Grammar, authorized by Henry VIII, and the colloquies of Erasmus and Corderius). Latin speech and letter-writing were, of course, very important, if not the most important accomplishments that a grammar school could teach in the sixteenth and early seventeenth centuries – hence, among other things, the wide reading of Terence, and the Westminster School Latin Play. With the later seventeenth and early eighteenth centuries these vocational objectives disappeared, and the compulsory use of Latin in speech was gradually dropped in schools, together with Corderius' and Erasmus' *Colloquies*, and the study of Cicero's correspondence. The classical languages, which throughout this period remained virtually the sole subject of instruction in schools, were now necessary to anyone who wished to understand the literature and participate in the elegances of social intercourse enjoyed by the upper classes; and the main activity in the curriculum was the writing of Latin verses and the reading of Roman poets. What happened to Classics in the nineteenth century we have already briefly discussed at the beginning of this chapter. Until the beginning of the nineteenth century the techniques of teaching elementary Latin changed little, apart from the decay of spoken Latin. Lily's Latin Grammar, slightly modified and renamed *The Eton Latin Grammar,* was used well into the nineteenth century and then superseded by *Kennedy's Latin Primer*, about which a Professor of General Linguistics wrote in 1951 'numerous resemblances in method and composition strike the eye of anyone who compares it [Priscian's *Institutiones Grammaticae*] with our own standard text

31

book, Kennedy's *Latin Primer'*. And throughout all these centuries the early stages of learning continued to be associated with uncongenial grind and physical violence. An American Jesuit scholar has compared the learning of Latin from the Renaissance onwards to a puberty rite, by which the young male was taught, to the accompaniment of pain, to dissociate himself from the infants and females of his family and take on the manly traditions of his tribe. The analogy is sufficiently plausible to amuse the sociologists and find a place in a sociological Reader on Education and History.

This teaching of Latin had been criticized by, amongst others, Milton, Comenius and Locke. A few individual teachers made experiments, but no systematic attempt was made to reform the teaching of elementary Latin before the beginning of the twentieth century, and then the attempt was treated with hostility and contempt by the leading schoolmasters and scholars of the day. Perhaps this is not surprising. Methods which can claim the authority of twenty centuries begin to seem grounded in the facts of nature. The traditions of classical education have been to praise rather than to emulate the experimental daring of the early Greeks and their emancipation from the authority of the past. As recently as 1973 the precepts of Quintilian were publicly invoked by a Classics teacher of note to anathematize the new methods of the Cambridge Latin Course!

The Direct Method

Romans of the Classical period learnt to speak Greek from their household slaves before they began to study it as a literary language. Dialogues were learnt by heart and repeated orally by the pupils of Bede and Alcuin. Up to the beginning of the eighteenth century many pupils were forbidden, on pain of punishment, to speak any language but Latin in school. There is a disrespectful Maupassant story of a nineteenth-century schoolmaster who taught Latin, with success, as a spoken language. But the systematic, contrived and persistent use of spoken Latin as a pedagogic device for learning literary Latin was an invention of the present century, and largely due to one man, W. H. D. Rouse, Headmaster of the Perse School, Cambridge, from 1902 to 1928, and University Teacher of Sanskrit. He enjoyed the collaboration of two of his assistant teachers, R. B. Appleton and W. H. S. Jones, Jones being concurrently both a teacher at the Perse School and a Classical Fellow and Tutor of St Catharine's College, Cambridge.

The history of the Latin Direct Method in England is both instructive and, in some degree, tragic. Towards the end of the nineteenth century there was a European movement for the abandonment of the grammar/translation ('La plume de ma tante') method in favour of an oral method of teaching modern foreign languages. It was pioneered by such eminent philologists as Henry Sweet (Shaw's 'Professor Higgins') and Otto Jespersen, and in France it was supported by the Ministry of Public Instruction. Many titles were canvassed for the new method; none fully comprehended its techniques, but 'Direct' was finally adopted as drawing attention to the total or partial elimination of the mother tongue as the medium of instruction and therefore bridge – or barrier – between the target language and the objects or actions it was denoting. Rouse transferred the aims and methods to the teaching of Latin and Greek. Like many revolutionaries he claimed not to be innovating but to be leading a return to the healthy practices of our ancestors, which had been perverted by the malign influence of German scholarship (the scapegoat, at one time or another, for most that has been thought wrong with Classics in England). Like many revolutionaries he was, in fact, distorting history, and he was doing less than justice to the great classical teachers of the nineteenth century who had swept away the obsolete relics of spoken Latin; but the distortion was in a good cause.

Rouse was an innovator of great energy and resourcefulness and an accomplished scholar, as was Jones. The Perse lessons were models of liveliness, involvement and economy of time. Not only did the Perse boys enjoy their Latin, many of them became scholars of Cambridge colleges and won Classical Firsts. The Board of Education published in 1910 a report (submitted by Rouse in fulfilment of the Board's conditions for a financial grant the Perse School had received) which included specimens (selected by the Board as typical) of the pupils' translations and compositions, both prose and verse. These were impressive by any standards. This was a time when the recently introduced School Certificate of the Oxford and Cambridge Board was revealing a very low level of attainment (considering the years of study involved) by large numbers of the entrants from public and grammar schools.

Why, then, did the Direct Method not succeed in superseding a method which was notoriously repugnant to the learners and was now being shown up as – for the average pupil – inefficient? The answer illustrates the once neglected truth that teaching does not take place in a social vacuum. The prestige of the major public schools was at its height in 1910 and they were in a position to dictate attitudes towards teaching and towards scholarship. A schoolmaster should be a gentleman and a scholar. Professionalism, methodology and teacher-training were for the elementary school teachers, who were neither. The Perse School was not a public school in the strict definition – a boarding school for the sons of the upper classes – and Rouse lacked the manner and personality to impress the educational establishment. It was not possible to put on a plausible, let alone a successful, performance with Direct Method without a rigorous apprenticeship and a fluency in spoken Latin. (It is now considered advisable for anyone proposing to teach a modern foreign language by an oral method to have at least six months of residence in the country where that language is spoken.) Rouse recommended a walking tour with a friend who is prepared to speak nothing but Latin for a week. However, Englishmen were traditionally insular and self-conscious about speaking any language but their own, when not compelled by circumstances. To ask them to speak Latin, where their training had done everything to inhibit them against risking grammatical solecisms, was inviting them to become ridiculous.

Teaching is, at the best of times, a conservative profession, and there are two necessary conditions for radical change to take place. First, an educational crisis to create a sense of acute dissatisfaction or insecurity among teachers. Second, the means for institutionalizing the change. It is instructive to make a comparison between the failure of Direct Method Latin to take root, and the speed with which the radically innovating Cambridge Latin Course has been widely adopted. In the case of the Cambridge Latin Course there has been the Schools Council to sponsor it and to add substantially to the funds supplied by its original patron, the Nuffield Foundation, and to encourage the Southern Universities Joint Examining Board to provide a tailor-made O-level. There was also JACT, with a Council containing respectable members of the public schools and the older universities (not that these now exercise anything like the influence they did in 1910), to publicize its aims and methods. But, above all, there was the crisis of comprehensivization which made obsolete many of the traditional assumptions about education, and threatened to eliminate the teaching of Latin in the maintained and voluntary-aided schools unless Latin could acquire a more attractive image.

The Direct Method attempted to institutionalize itself in The Association for the Reform of Latin Teaching. The Summer School at which this was formed was attended by 200 teachers, and another day-school of good standing (Whitgift) was enthusiastically committed to Direct Method. The tragedy was that this took place in 1913. When the Association next met at a Summer School in 1919 the two Direct Method teachers from Whitgift were dead, and so were many other young men who might have had the enterprise to undertake the new methods. The ARLT came to be regarded as the poor man's Classical Association and was cold-shouldered by scholars and public school-masters (with a few honourable exceptions). The method was taken up by a number of teachers in grammar schools, convent or private schools, some of whom had the enthusiasm but lacked the skill, or the drive, or the dedication of the pioneers, and brought it into disrepute for failing to produce the skills of accurate and fluent translation and composition — which the traditional methods equally failed to produce in all but the best pupils — or even that rudimentary knowledge of elementary

Latin grammar which the traditional methods could at least claim to teach by dint of much rote-learning. There was no tailor-made examination for the Direct Method and, apart from the Board of Education's small grant, no public funds for organizing training courses and validatory surveys, or for paying Research and Development Officers.

After the Second World War there was a revival of interest in Direct Method, brought about through the publication of two clever new course books by a pupil and a pupil of a pupil of Rouse: but many of the teachers who bought these books used them for basically non-oral teaching.

Observations on the Direct Method

We teach Latin so that our pupils may read Latin literature; that is now generally agreed. But this creates a dilemma. When you begin to read literary texts with your pupils, do you regard the lesson as a language lesson, in which your first considerations are of increasing the fluency of your pupils and their mastery of linguistic forms; or do you consider it a literature lesson in which your duty is to enable your pupils to appreciate the text to their fullest capacity? The two objectives are seldom in harmony. It might be thought at first that they are in harmony in a Rousean lesson where the text can be discussed *in Latin* (or Greek); but this is not so. Someone once asked flippantly what the Latin was for 'er . . . um'. The question has its serious side. We cannot reconstruct Roman colloquial speech. Plautus and Terence are as much and as little help as Sheridan or Pinter would be for reconstructing English colloquial speech. And yet large-scale investigations conducted for the French audio/lingual courses at St Cloud showed that 'fillers' (the French fillers were *oh, ah, quoi!, eh bien*) are of high frequency in conversation. When television and radio critics need to employ such fillers as 'I mean', 'sort of', 'you know', 'in the last analysis' how much more needful must such expressions be to far less articulate pupils who are tentatively putting into words their half-understood responses to a text! The oral teaching of the Middle Ages and the Renaissance took place in schools where Latin was spoken in all classrooms and, no doubt slangily, outside the classrooms. Lacking this background of habitual unself-conscious use, Direct Method Latin, save in the hands of unusually resourceful and histrionically gifted teachers, is always in danger of becoming fossilized into stereotyped drills in which language has quite lost touch with reality; especially when the Direct Method course has been constructed round a grammar (Priscian/Kennedy) which is more interested in analysis at word-level than at sentence-level. To expect Latin to be the vehicle for the discussion of pupils' reactions to a text and of the subtleties of intention and expression which the text reveals is asking too much at any stage. Mastery of Latin will always lag far behind the resources required for this aspect of teaching and how important this aspect is will be shown in the next chapter.

None the less, Direct Method has the great merit of treating language-learning as skill not knowledge, and it provides ample opportunity for *performance* as well as for *experience* of the language. We may not have heard the last of Direct (or audio/lingual) Method in Latin or Greek teaching yet.

Waldo Sweet and structural linguistics

Professor Waldo E. Sweet, of the William Penn Charter School in Phila-delphia, and later of the University of Michigan, actively recognized, long before anyone in Britain, that there was significance in modern linguistic theory for the teaching of Latin; and in *Latin: a Structural Approach* (1957) and *Artes Latinae* (1966–73) he produced teaching materials which strikingly departed from the traditional course books. The word 'structural', basic to many disciplines, has no absolutely fixed meaning in any of them. In American linguistics at the time that Sweet began his work it was associated with the name of Leonard Bloomfield and with language studies which concentrated on form and disregarded meaning – or, to be more precise, disregarded the contexts and functions of language in the lives of its users. Looking at Latin in the role of a structural analyst, Sweet was forcibly struck by the degree of its formal difference from English; a difference regularly disguised or minimized by most course books, which offered, for practice in read-ing and translation, specimens of 'Latin' constructed (by the authors of the course book) with a sequence of words which would be entirely appropriate for English, except that the verb was always to be recog-nized by its position at the end of the sentence. This is so uncharacteris-tic of Classical Latin that it led to great difficulty when the first authen-tic texts were encountered. It is a maxim of Applied Linguistics that the target language and the mother tongue of the learner should be contrastively analysed so that areas of difficulty and likely error can be predicted. On the principle that nettles should be grasped firmly, not gingerly, Sweet resolved that the contrast of inflection as against word-order should be emphasized from the start (the Cambridge Latin Course has taken the opposite view). Formal analysis also allowed him to present initially the nominative and accusative of all nouns as effectively only two forms: the nominatives ending in -s or zero allomorph, and the accusatives in -m or zero allomorph, but this novel and interesting beginning soon gives way to the traditional categorization into five declensions, and structural analysis produces no further surprises. Ameri-can structural linguistics was associated with behaviourist psychology, and, in his introduction to *Latin*, Sweet quotes 'A famous authority on language' as saying that effective language learning means over-learning (i.e. learning that can be recalled without hesitation or thought). On these grounds Sweet used for his course 360 *sententiae*, of greater or less profundity, culled from twelve centuries of Latin, varying from three to twelve words in length, eked out by a number of brief 'narrative readings', mainly fables or epigrams. The *sententiae* serve, with mutations, to illustrate the morphological or syntactic lesson to be learnt; to provide matter for batteries of elucidatory questions of the Direct Method type; and for exercises ('pattern practice') in transformation, repetition, substitution and expansion. In 1958 a celebrated article on Teaching Machines, by the behaviourist psychologist B. F. Skinner, converted Sweet into an adherent of programmed learning. *Artes Latinae* is an adaptation and development of the ideas underlying *Latin* to fit Skinner's theory of operant conditioning (i.e. that the learner shall be carried forward from task to task by immediate re-inforcement — the satisfaction of getting the answer right). This demands the breakdown of the learning into very small stages ('molecularization') of a rigorously hierarchical process.

Observations on Waldo Sweet

Only a competent student of linguistics could usefully criticize the quality of Sweet's linguistic analyses and explanations; and it is always rash for anyone who has not seen a course in action to express an opinion on it — especially when *experts* have not always been proved right in their predictions about language laboratories, teaching machines and primary school French. However, certain things can be said. In *Latin* Sweet does not follow his own precepts. He adjures the teacher to keep talk *about* the language to a minimum, as students will learn Latin by hearing it, speaking it, reading it and writing it, *not* by talking about it. Excellent advice! Yet he is constantly telling his students *about* Latin, and about contrastive language patterns in Aztec, Navaho, Ilamba, Mongbandi and many other languages. Before the student can start at all he has to digest *phoneme, morpheme, morphology*; and in Lesson One he meets *allomorphs* and *zero allomorphs*. Chicken feed, perhaps, to the American student, but an English pupil would find it hard to assimilate all the knowledge offered to him. In the teaching of modern languages recognition of the value of Phonetics resulted, for a period of time, in the intrusion of Phonetics teaching into the classroom. Its place is now recognized to be more properly in the training of the teacher. In *Latin*, Linguistics seems similarly to have intruded into the classroom almost against Sweet's own better judgment. A more serious objection is that until Lesson 22 the only Latin that has been met are little nuggets offered in a contextual vacuum. Excellent nuggets some of them are and perhaps deserve rather more respect than they receive. *Non in solo pane vivit homo* springs the question, *Quo auxilio homo non alitur?* To which the student is expected to reply, *Pane solo*. Other nuggets are more classical but more banal, as *Suum cuique pulchrum est*, or *Non ovum tam simile ovo*.

What is one to say of *Artes Latinae*? It describes itself in the introduction to the first teacher's manual as a 'total program for the teaching of Latin', and indeed, with the fifty-four tapes, five sound films, twenty-two study prints, test booklets, graded readers, reference notebooks and so forth, one feels that totality could hardly go further. By the end of the first half of the course the 'expected terminal behavior' includes 'the ability to read and understand Latin literature without recourse to English; positive attitudes towards the study of Latin, foreign languages, and intellectual pursuits in general; and improvement of study habits'. Finally one is told that the text was tested and rewritten until it was 'successful with most high school students who used it'.

Sweet has written in *Didaskalos* that between writing his first materials and composing *Artes Latinae* he discovered that 'language learning is *both* automatic acquisition of habits *and* problem solving'. This was an opportune discovery for anyone proposing to write a programmed course, since presenting a problem (the stimulus) for solution (the response) fits very neatly into the pattern required. What does not fit the pattern so easily is hearing the language, speaking it, reading it and writing it in a *meaningful context*, to cull a phrase from modern language teaching.

The Cambridge Latin Course

The temptation to an English teacher of Latin, on looking at *Artes Latinae*, is to be excessively sceptical that a technique based on experiments with rats and pigeons will work when humans are substituted for animals and symbolic ticks and crosses for food pellets and electric shocks. With the Cambridge Latin Course the temptation is to be too uncritical, inasmuch as it has undoubtedly saved Latin from extinction in many comprehensive schools. True, this may sometimes have occurred because it was 'new and exciting' rather than for its real merits; but once adopted it had to justify itself to keep its place.

Perse Direct Method can only be properly studied through the writings, course books and teacher's guides of Rouse and his collaborators; and the monumental work of Waldo Sweet through his own copious writings. However, the Perse books are out of print, and Sweet's materials are very expensive and difficult to obtain in Britain, whereas the Cambridge Latin Course, though expensive, is not excessively expensive, and it is easy to obtain. No one who is interested in the teaching of Classics should omit to study this remarkable and revolutionary achievement through its materials and through the writings of those who created them. Here I will only draw attention to some of its most striking departures from tradition.

The project team which constructed the course included initially a linguistic consultant whose research programme into the applicability of contemporary linguistic theory to the teaching of a classical language provided the starting point for their work. He has outlined the sort of rigorous and comprehensive theoretical framework that he believes should underlie the design of a language-learning course. This should be treated, as far as possible, like the design of an aeroplane, despite the difference that the aeroplane, if constructed on a faulty hypothesis, will fall out of the sky; whereas a defective course, if fashionably dressed up and cleverly marketed, will continue to sell because the teachers using it are sure to blame their failures on the low intelligence of their pupils, the baneful influence of TV, comprehensivization or other readily available scapegoats. Research for the design and construction of a course, he stipulated, should begin from a detailed definition of the problem to be solved, a specification of the most suitable solution and a hypothesis to bridge the gap between the two. The definition should include criteria of relevance for collecting data on the problem, as well as a set of functional and formal objectives; the hypothesis should be predictive and *capable of validation*; and the solution should provide for feedback, and specify conditions for optimum operation. For a course in Latin or Classical Greek the functional objective would be threefold: '(1) An ability to process the surface information of unseen material up to the level of complexity reached. (2) A cultural component — something of the view of the outside world peculiar to the language. (3) Some literary appreciation of the conventions and artifices that are characteristic of the literature to be studied.'

Regretfully it must be admitted that if the Cambridge Latin Course were an aeroplane it would by now have fallen out of the sky. Nevertheless, in my opinion, it has transformed our notions of what a Latin course should be, and made obsolete all previous Latin courses; and its successes are far more remarkable than its failures. The reasons for its failure to achieve the rigorously high standards demanded by its linguistic consultant stem from the exigencies of time and money which made it impossible to construct a theoretical framework adequate for this demand. In particular, a major part of the hypothesis — that a pupil could, from a skilfully designed course, develop within three years an intuitive grammar, without the help of explicit grammar learning—was not made capable of validation in any precise sense; so we cannot say for certain why it is that many pupils are *not* proving capable of processing 'the surface information of unseen material up to the level of complexity reached'.

The first of the three parts of the functional objective is common to other courses. The other two parts would probably be considered desirable by other course writers, but the CLC is the first course to take them really seriously. This was made possible because it was written by a team who were continuously criticizing each other's efforts, and who showed a remarkable talent for constructing stories, well-characterized, well-constructed and very sophisticated — considering that they were working, for each story, within rigidly defined linguistic limits, and introducing sociological aspects on a predetermined plan, while restricting themselves to plots and situations which they felt would be near enough to the experience and understanding of thirteen- to fifteen-year-old pupils to engage their interest and their feelings. The writers themselves did a great deal of ferreting in historical and archaeological sources; they also had ready access to scholars who were experts in the relevant areas.

Previous courses had reckoned to teach the language first — usually with a jejune outline of Roman history thrown in; the language input being governed by a progression through the priscianic categories, and allowing for the expression — in the reading matter — of no more than trivialities. One well-known course deliberately left out the Roman history on the principle that only one difficulty — or one unknown — should be tackled at a time. This method of proceeding has, in part, been responsible for the shock of difficulty felt by most pupils when they embarked on their first Roman author. The CLC expects the pupil from the start to regard what he reads as worthy of discussion and criticism, both from the literary aspect and from the sociological. Without excessive flattery the CLC could be regarded as a preliminary to a course in both sociology and literary criticism. The aim is that the pupil shall not, when he comes to read Pliny and Tacitus, Catullus, Virgil and Ovid, feel lost in their cultural ambience, and shall be prepared to recognize the implicit meanings conveyed through the literary 'conventions and artifices' employed.

After the incursion into linguistics of B. F. Skinner, the next major development in American linguistics was the appearance of the generative/transformational theories of Noam Chomsky, who restored the study of meaning to a central place in linguistics. The CLC is linguistically eclectic. It owes little or nothing to the behaviourist theories of B. F. Skinner, but it owes much to structuralism in the wider sense that items of language are considered to have significance only through their relationship to all the other items in the total system of that language (just as individual chessmen owe all their significance to their relationship to all the other pieces in the game): and it owes much to transformational theories. The use it has made of linguistic insights from these sources show a very high degree of originality. It is sometimes thought that improved courses in Latin (or Greek) could be constructed by imitating this or that aspect of the CLC without imitating the process by which the CLC was produced. This would be surprising. The CLC is itself 'structuralist' in the sense that none of its parts functions independently of the others.

Observations on the Cambridge Latin Course

The most damaging charge against it is that its pupils do not develop an intuitive grammar of Latin sufficiently effective to enable them to read unseen texts even of modest difficulty. This is a damaging charge because the course specifically sets out to do this. Nevertheless, I hold the heterodox view that it is not a crushing charge (if proven). For the four out of five pupils who give up their Latin when they have done their O-level, what is important is *to have read and appreciated* some Latin literature, not the possession of the skill to read other Latin literature at some time in the future. Mottoes, gravestones, honorific inscriptions and literary tags are all the Latin that most people encounter in their adult lives unless they go looking for it, and then they can take a Loeb with them. None the less something has gone wrong. Is the theory of language acquisition on which the course is based misconceived in whole or in part? Perhaps, yet there is still the possibility that the theory is correct but the construction of the course faulty, or that teachers have not yet discovered the best way of teaching it. Most teachers are reacting to their failures with the course by supplementing it with formal grammar teaching, carefully fed into its stages and reinforced by varied linguistic exercises in substitution, manipulation, parsing and gap-filling. Thus when the intuitive grammar fails, the pupil will, it is hoped, be able to fall back on sentence analysis of the traditional kind; which is, surely, the way that most of us behave who have progressed beyond the stage of construe to fluent reading, but not so fluent that we are not checked from time to time by the less lucid sentences of Tacitus or the more tightly packed lines of Horace. Some teachers are even incorporating English-Latin translation into their course, on the pedagogic principle that an adequate amount of *performance* in the language should be required of their pupils relative to the amount of *experience* they receive in it.

There are, of course, teachers who have despaired and regressed to traditional methods, or compromised with *Ecce Romani.* Whether they are wise to do so, or not, must depend on what their objectives and priorities are. The gain is likely to include relief from that cold sweat that breaks out on a teacher's brow when his O-level class, in some trouble with Aeneas' exordium to the tale of Troy, are pressed to look carefully at word endings, and announce with aggrieved self-righteousness that *incipiam* can *only* be a Category 1 noun in Form B singular. On the other hand there will be the loss of the lively interest created by the cleverly designed characters and plots and the unfamiliar assumptions of the society in which they operate. The teacher will also lose the sense of reassurance that whether or not his pupils ever pass O-level or translate Latin unseen, they are, at least, receiving more insight into Roman society than came the way of most successful O-level candidates on the old dispensation.

A very experienced teacher, who has taught the CLC for as many years as it has been going, reports on it thus:

> A Grade 1 in the CLC (SUBJ) O-level is no guarantee of success at A-level (as A-level Latin is at present examined). The fruits of the CLC become more clearly apparent when the time comes for Oxbridge entrance. By then most candidates have, by sheer accumulation of time spent on reading, reached an adequate standard of translation, while they show a much enhanced ability in General Papers, where they can and do answer questions from their own experience and reactions. Their success with questions on education, slavery, religion, economics and so forth is most noticeable. The beginnings of this are traceable to the early stages of the course as well as to the 'bridge' reading and the texts.

It should perhaps be mentioned that this teacher has a generous allowance of time for his course. Latin has been shown by the statisticians to be more difficult than *any other subject* at O-level and headmasters who think they have solved their moral dilemmas by squeezing it into two years or a meagre three are guilty of cowardice, carelessness or ignorance.

The teaching of Greek

All languages are equal in the eyes of God and of the general linguists; so one must never suggest that there is anything special about classical Greek. It is therefore necessary to look first for extrinsic reasons for the peculiar enthusiasm generated by the teaching and learning of Greek. The Joint Association of Classical Teachers has been for the last twelve years organizing a Greek Summer School to which a steadily growing number of school pupils come voluntarily to work very hard for a fortnight of their holidays. They come again, and, if allowed, yet again (and so do the teachers). The extrinsic reasons can hardly be material, as a knowledge of classical Greek has small value in the employment market and no longer leads to deaneries and episcopal palaces. The pleasure in learning Greek stems largely, no doubt, from the charm or the power of the literature that is quickly accessible to the learner. Pupils who come to the Summer School knowing no more Greek than the alphabet read, before the end of their fortnight, some Homer and some passages from Greek tragedy. A cynic, arguing from press reports of the Summer Schools, might say that the pleasure stems from the esoteric state of the subject; that Greek learning has become a kind of intellectually respectable rosicrucianism. Like many cynical misrepresentations this arguably contains a small grain of truth. An obstinate believer in intrinsic value might put forward the theory that literary Greek, as developed during the centuries from Homer to Hecataeus, reflected the realities of social life among the Ionian aristocrats, who were quarrelsome, arrogant and selfish but gifted with a rare taste for poetry and song and intellectual stimulation; that the poets and prose writers of the archaic age bequeathed to their successors a language whose potentialities they had exploited as brilliantly as the sculptors had exploited the potentialities of Parian or Pentelic marble to make it a language of singular grace and limpidity. No doubt the linguists would say that this is nothing but a northerners' fantasy derived from association of the language with imaginary vistas of dazzling white marble, triremes rippling through the blue Mediterranean, supple limbs in the palaestra, roses and wine and a healthy freedom from Asiatic sense of sin and Nordic preoccupation with guilt. Perhaps, more specifically, one could claim that the Greek writers discovered the uses of their inflected article in combination with the participial and infinitival forms of their verbs to express quite subtle and complex ideas with apparent simplicity and without recourse to clinical abstractions. This use of untechnical language to discuss problems of philosophy or politics, and the lack of words specially coined to encapsulate organizing concepts or syntheses of characteristic data (see p. 67), hampered intellectual progress. But in the modern world, where this language has found its way into the vocabulary of popular journalists and every pseudo-intellectual, an encounter with the apparent simplicity of Greek philosophical language has often the charm of an unexpected encounter with rather exquisite good manners.

Be all this as it may, Greek as a school subject is showing great tenacity in very unfavourable circumstances.

Innovatory courses in Greek

In the Renaissance, Greek was taught in and through Latin. This did not deter Rouse from developing a full-blooded Greek Direct Method course. Its final achievement was to inspire Peckett and Munday — pupils of the first and second generation — to write *Thrasymachus*, by general agreement the best Greek course book for use in English schools at the moment. A new course is now in preparation by a team chosen and advised by the Greek committee of JACT and financed by funds raised by their appeal. This course will certainly be much influenced by both the successes and the failures of the CLC. It will be aimed at Sixth Forms rather than at the middle school.

Greek has, like Latin, attracted the attentions of students of structural linguistics, and courses have emanated from both McGill University and the Massachusetts Institute of Technology. These are constructed on somewhat similar lines to Sweet's structuralist *Latin*, and they both make much use of pattern practice designed for the language laboratory.

On pronunciation

Apart from the Greek accentual system, the Greek and Roman grammarians did not create an apparatus of phonetics with which to describe the sounds of their language in speech; though a number of phonetic observations are to be found in their works. It is from these and from other, accidental, clues that modern philologists have partially reconstructed the pronunciation of Latin and Greek — vowel and consonant values with some confidence, but sentence intonations hardly at all. The way that Greek and Latin have been pronounced in England over the centuries is an interesting part of linguistic history, involving the influences of Byzantine refugees, Norman schoolmasters, the writings of Erasmus, sixteenth-century religious politics, the great English vowel-shift, misguided Dutch scholarship and the efforts of the Classical Association. After the use of spoken Latin had disappeared from the classroom few teachers paid heed to the sound of the ancient languages and Direct Method teachers first began through the ARLT the uphill struggle to raise standards of pronunciation. Sad to relate, even now the pronunciation of the average schoolmaster or schoolmistress is inconsistent, inaccurate and corrupted by the sounds of modern English. He, or she, is apt to consider the pronunciation of a dead language as unimportant. Gilbert Murray wrote somewhere that he too might have thought it unimportant had he not, at some time during his Australian boyhood, had the experience of being taught French poetry by a schoolmaster who had never heard the sounds of French. The Latin and Greek literatures were composed for the ear rather than for the eye, and should be heard by pupils as well as seen. If the teacher learns to speak and read the language consistently, and as accurately as he can, his pupils will not need too much correction to be induced to do likewise; otherwise slovenliness will be perpetuated and there will be an unnecessary source of confusion in the early stages. Besides it is difficult to correct gross defects when the ear has once become habituated to them.

In England, since the eighteenth century, Greek accents have been written, but ignored in pronunciation by most scholars and teachers.

There is today controversy among experts as to whether the tonic – or pitch – accentual system denoted by the Greek accents, could be reproduced by English speakers. Among those (the majority) who do not think so, there is support for the practice (general in Germany and the USA) of pronouncing them as stress accents. This has the advantage that it facilitates the subsequent learning of Modern Greek. A few schoolteachers go so far as to train their pupils to pronounce Classical Greek with the consonant and vowel sounds as well as with the accentuation of Modern Greek. This still further facilitates the subsequent learning of Modern Greek; but the abolition of the distinctions of vowel length, which came with conversion of the Classical Greek pitch accent to the Byzantine Greek stress accent, must excessively distort the sound of Classical Greek prose and, still more, of Classical Greek verse.

Scansion

If pupils have been taught from their first lessons to read accurately and with a feeling for the meaning of what they are reading, they can be taught to read verse well. *After* they can do that, *not before*, is the time to initiate them into an analysis of metre, in so far as this is necessary at all. A knowledge of Greek and Latin metrical laws is neither a necessary nor a sufficient cause for a pupil to read well, though it will certainly help him to read better if he already does read well.

On prose composition

This chapter cannot be completed without some discussion of this highly controversial subject. Prose composition in Latin and Greek was a pedagogic invention of Victorian schoolmasters, Arnold of Rugby in particular. They substituted it for the writing of Themes – free compositions on a set subject, an exercise that went back to the schools of Greece and Rome. The Theme had become either a facile exercise in manipulating a number of well-worn Latin clichés or (as set by Thomas Arnold) it strained the resources of the Sixth Form pupil's Latinity and compared ill with the English essay as a vehicle for original thinking. The choice of memorable passages from masters of English prose to be translated into the Latin of Cicero, Livy or Tacitus, or the Greek of Demosthenes, Plato or Thucydides, had the double advantage that it familiarized the pupil with some fine specimens of English prose and presented him with a worthwhile intellectual challenge.

There are, nowadays, critics who regard the exercise of prose composition as overrated and slightly ridiculous. They claim that not even the most accomplished scholar could be sure that his compositions would not appear to an educated Roman or Greek as comic as 'Babu English' — the literary English of the Indian clerks of the Indian Civil Service in the heyday of the Raj. This writing seemed comic to supercilious Englishmen because, though founded on some knowledge of literary English, its use of metaphor and simile was uncontrolled by a familiarity with colloquial English which would have checked extravagance of the 'Hand that rocked the cradle has kicked the bucket' type. Certainly, as practised in Classical education, composition in prose (and verse) is a species of pastiche, but the comparison with 'Babu English' is unfair and misleading, as that arose from insensitive and uncritical reading of literary English. Excellent literary English is written today by Indians and others who have never held a conversation with a native English speaker. Anyhow, if the exercise is worth while as a pastiche, we need not fear the resuscitation of Demosthenes or Cicero to mock our efforts. But is it worth while? The debate often confuses issues which are theoretical with those which are practical. It might be possible to say that prose composition is theoretically of great value, but in the circumstances prevailing in schools and universities today it can no longer be performed at a level where it achieves that value — either not at all, or only by sacrificing other studies of even greater value.

What are the values that can be claimed for prose composition? The fact that Latin and Greek are fusional (or inflectional) languages, whereas English is a blend of isolating, fusional and agglutinative (in other words, the fact that the two languages employ quite different methods of signalling meaning), requires a writer (in theory, at least), when he is transferring ideas from one language to the other, to undertake some sort of transformational exercise, from the surface structure of one language to a deep structure and back to the surface structure of the other. The value of this exercise would be to lay the foundations of linguistic perceptiveness — though it could not be claimed as a first stage in a training in linguistics unless the analyses were made explicit. Perhaps a more convincing claim can be made at the level of cultural contrast. The outlook on the world and the unexamined assumptions of members of a society which is post-Christian and industrialized will necessarily become explicit when ideas from the literature of that society have to be expressed in language which would have meaning for a reader in a pre-Christian, pre-industrial society. Explicating the concepts that underlie the language being translated could be a valuable exercise in conceptual analysis. There is a third point — the nature of literary Latin. The logicality of the Latin language (paralleled by the contractual outlook of the Roman religion) as the expression of the organizing genius of the Roman people, though claimed as recently as 1928 by the eminent French linguist A. Meillet, is now (like the grace and limpidity of Greek) a concept so unacceptable to linguistic scholars that it is perhaps best forgotten; but the conscious development of literary Latin as the vehicle of oratory, by students of Greek rhetorical theory, with the aim of achieving clarity of expression as an essential for public debate — this is a process which has been charted by philologists, and shows a steadily increasing precision in expressing the articulation of ideas in those famous subordinate clauses and ablative absolutes. In other words, some things which can be left ambiguous in English must be made explicit in Ciceronian prose.

All of which is not to say that the ability to write a Latin prose is 'incompatible with confusion of thought'; or that it is not possible to learn clarity of expression at the expense of having very little to say that is worth expressing clearly; or that it is sensible to condemn as slipshod the writing of some contemporary whose views one dislikes simply on the grounds that it would not go easily into Latin; or that putting into Latin the already Latinate prose of the eighteenth century, or simple narrative prose of any century, can be called an exercise involving a high degree of intellectual rigour.

Chapter four

On teaching the classical literatures

'I am painfully aware by bitter experience that I cannot give you any idea of the passion, the power, the essential guts of the lines which you have so foully outraged in my presence. But insofar as in me lies, I will strive to bring home to you, Vernon, the fact that there exist in Latin a few pitiful rules of grammar, of syntax, nay even of declension, which were not created for your incult sport — your Boeotian diversion.'

'Mr King' in Rudyard Kipling's *Regulus: an ode of Horace*

Virgil is a cold-hearted bore.

Bernard Levin in *The Times*, 1974

The duty of education . . . is not merely to add to, but in some respects to counteract the acquirements of infancy and childhood. Up to this period the boy has been accustomed to regard, in the stores of romance which form his present treasure, the meaning only and not the language — the substance and not the form. His Ovid and his Xenophon, his Virgil and his Homer are regarded from the opposite point of view. He is made now to take cognizance of the forms rather than the substance. Thus his mind is enabled to conceive form as an object of thought, distinct from the subject matter and vice versa. It must be allowed . . . that a young boy can be brought to take but a feeble interest in the metamorphoses of Lycaon and Daphne, the trials of pius Aeneas, the up-country marches of Cyrus or even the wrath of Achilles. The reason is that his whole attention is centred on the language, the difficulties of which requiring to be mastered step by step compel him to proceed so slowly as to lose all interest in the story.

The Rev. W. G. Clarke, 1855

The notion, often met with nowadays, that a work should be considered independently of its author is justified only in so far as the work often gives a truer, more integrated picture of its creator than do the sometimes fortuitous and misleading bits of information that we possess concerning his life. In order to discern the proper relation between an artist's life and his work, a critic requires experience of his own, discretion, and an open-mindedness based on a thorough knowledge of the material. In any event, what we understand and love in a work is a human existence, a possibility of 'modifications' within ourselves.

Erich Auerbach, *Literary language and its Public*, 1958

Preamble

An eminent professor of the Philosophy of Education, when discussing the theory that education is properly the education of reason, expressed the belief that reason in the educated man should be associated with passion, and one of the forms that this passion should take is a hatred of inaccuracy and slovenliness. Such hatred of slovenliness, he feels, was a valuable product of the 'old' classical teaching, and liable to disappear — the baby with the bath-water — in the 'new'. He describes a visit to an American school in which he witnessed a lesson centred on the well-known letter of Pliny the Younger about the boy and the dolphin. In the lesson no effort was spared to relate the subject of the Latin text to the pupils' interests. In particular, reference was made to a visiting baseball team called 'The Dolphins', whose performance was discussed at length. Finally the Latin text was scampered through with such haste that it remained an open question whether the pupils had more than the haziest idea of what Pliny's Latin was, in detail, saying (the children would feel rejected if their mistakes were pointed out, the teacher explained); let alone that ability to analyse his sentences and their component parts which would have been required by a rigorous application of the 'old' methods of Classics teaching.

This story (apart from showing to what absurd lengths a teacher can go who considers the learning of Latin to be a bitter pill which can only be administered if coated with an inordinate amount of sugar) raises some interesting questions in the light of the professor's views on the value of Latin. Is it, for instance, a major function of a lesson on a Pliny letter, or of any Latin lesson, to teach a hatred of slovenliness? Does precise attention to linguistic detail in Latin transfer itself to linguistic precision in other languages? And, further, to precision in general intellectual behaviour? These are questions on which there is no conclusive evidence. For example — if one may illustrate the point fictionally — did 'Vernon' become, *as the result of the Latin teaching of Mr King to the army class* (of which 'Vernon' is a member), a soldier notable for precise attention to the details of his professional work? Are classical

49

scholars more than averagely scrupulous in verifying their references and checking their proofs; and if so, could this not be so because an inherited capacity for attention to detail has drawn them to Classics? Attempts to answer this sort of question have not yet been very successful.

More important, in a chapter on the teaching of literature, are questions about the nature of the accuracy inculcated by the 'old' methods. Pliny's letter is not simply a chunk of Latin language. It is a letter; but what sort of a letter, with its rhetorical polish and neatly turned sentences? Did Pliny really expect his friend Caninius to write a poem about the tragic dolphin? We know that the story is a conflation of several stories; what guided the choice of the incidents and the invention of extra details? Pliny says the story is true; does he really mean this, and if so, what is his criterion of truth? Answers to all these questions can be attempted from a study of the text; they are interesting and stimulating questions, and unless they have been at least considered the text has been very superficially studied. But (exceptional teachers apart) none of these questions would have been raised by the 'old' classical teaching, which was only too often rigorous merely about the surface meaning, but incurious about the nature of the text as a piece of literature.

Why teach classical literature?

The Ionian aristocrats for whom Homer composed his songs, the associates of Sappho and Alcaeus who sang and listened to their lyrics, the Athenian audiences who witnessed the first performances of the *Oresteia*, the *Antigone*, or the *Medea*, required, one supposes, no schoolmasters to tell them what the poets meant and how listeners should respond to their creations. But by the Hellenistic age schoolteachers and scholars had become indispensable if each new generation were to become aware of the thought and art of the classical masters. To judge from the evidence assembled in Marrou's *History of Education in Antiquity*, the schoolteachers of both Greece and Rome discharged their task with rigorous pedantry. Teaching literature meant teaching an exhaustive fund of philological and mythological lore which any modern educationist would scarify as certain to kill any capacity for the enjoyment of literature however promising. But for the Greek or Roman pupil there was no escape onto a Science side; a deep familiarity with classical literature was ingrained into him as a matter of course. It is not unreasonable to suspect that the pleasure taken in a close knowledge of the great writers was sometimes akin to intellectual snobbery. There seems, at any rate, to have been no question of opting out of the literary culture. Until the rise of the soldier emperors of the late empire, membership of the governing classes was unthinkable without it; wealthy freedmen were mocked for lacking it; even Christians found it necessary to acquire it, rooted though it was in paganism. And nobody seems to have asked very searchingly why literary culture was so necessary.

Today only too many people are liable to ask why literary culture is necessary, and to reject it without waiting for an answer. It is possible to have some sympathy for them. We have most of us at some time known persons of deep literary culture, to whom literature was more vivid than life, for whom the first signs of spring would predictably evoke *Atalanta in Calydon*, and the chill of autumn *quam multae glomerantur aves* ·... , or Milton's Vallombrosa. Such people were mocked by H. G. Wells as being unable to hear a skylark without raining quotations from Shelley, or to see a three-legged stool without exclaiming 'Ah Delphi!'. In the last century of the Roman Empire an exclusively literary and rhetorical education produced aristocrats who spent their time in literary trifling when they would have been much better employed in helping the emperors to grapple with the catastrophes that were overwhelming civilization. Had they been trained as economists or sociologists or been graduates of Strategic Studies, they might have been of much greater use to the tottering empire. But a mind well-furnished with classical literary culture does not necessarily inhibit a man from effective action, nor from intellectual vigour and originality (nor, as George Steiner has observed, does it necessarily prevent him from being a cold-blooded Gestapo sadist). None the less, Wells was not without some justification in believing that to be steeped in classical literature might incline a man to see present reality out of focus, prejudice him against new ways of experiencing life, and disable him from acknowledging and appreciating anything good in social or technological change. Hence one of the many sources of hostility towards Classics on the part of militants for social and intellectual progress. However, since Classics has been so energetically deposed from its central position in education, there is little fear now of anyone getting *steeped* in classical literature in school. Is there, then, a value in getting a mere tincture? Perhaps.

Our perceptions of reality are not like the passive receptivity of the camera film. How we see and experience the outside world is controlled by our values, attitudes and beliefs. For most of us these are an unsystematic miscellany derived from religious belief, popular science, journalism, literature, television or the films — in a word, from the myths of our times. These are liable to be tainted by commercialism or by narrowly sectarian politics, to be crude and provincial, and distorted by transient obsessions. The strong argument for literary education is that provinciality is counteracted by classical literature, whether it be Homer, Sophocles and Virgil or Shakespeare, Milton and Keats. Classical authors are of another age as well as transcending all ages. But if they are to counteract provincialism they must be felt, not merely encountered; and felt deeply enough to be taken into the pupils' mythological miscellany in competition with the seductive offerings of the modern media of communication. Dealing as he does with pupils who are subject to a bombardment of the perceptions, a classical schoolteacher must nowadays be patient, sensitive and resourceful if the reading of classical authors in class is to prove more than a series of casual encounters.

The problems

1 The language: a dilemma

By and large a pupil learns to read Greek and Latin literature by reading Greek and Latin literature. Hence the dilemma mentioned in the last chapter. Is the reading of a Latin or Greek text to be a language lesson, designed to increase fluency in the language as used by Thucydides or Virgil in order to facilitate further reading; or is it to be a literary experience designed to cultivate the understanding and appreciation of the particular piece of literature being read (and, by extension, to illuminate all literature to be read in the future)?

There is no happy escape from the dilemma. The only possible course is to read sometimes quite rapidly, touching lightly on the literary aspects of the text, and in other lessons to lavish time on a thorough consideration of the text in the way that it would be treated by an English teacher who had no worries about his pupils' fluency in reading the language.

Another aspect of the same problem is pinpointed by the quotation from Clarke: the story. When the text is part of an epic or a tragedy, to pause for a slow analysis of an episode is to halt the very development of the drama from which the episode acquires its full meaning. *Hamlet*, taken twenty lines at a time, would make a limited impact on a reader; and the traditional pace of reading Greek tragedy and Roman epic has meant that even when the beauty of the trees had been admired, their contribution to the total beauty of the wood remained unperceived.

However, despair is not necessary. Kipling says of the Latin teacher on whom he modelled his 'Mr King' that though he taught him 'to loathe Horace for two years; to forget him for twenty' he had still taught him thereafter 'to love him for the rest of my days and through many sleepless nights'. There seems to be no good reason why we should not do better than Mr King.

2 The cultural barriers

No Greek author whose work has survived quite resembled the Chinese poet Po-chu'i, who, we are told, read his poems to his old servant and altered anything she could not understand; and so far from writing for simple-minded old servants, the Roman authors wrote for highly sophisticated readers who had been educated in Greek literature and derived much of their enjoyment from the demands made on them by the allusive and elliptical techniques of their poets and the 'resonance' effected by creative imitation of Greek and Roman antecedents.

Catullus is the first Roman author whom teachers dare to hope their pupils will enjoy. This is not because he wrote for unsophisticated adolescents, but because, though his techniques are subtle, the *persona* he projects is straightforward, uninhibited, impetuous and engagingly immature — very much as adolescents are likely to see themselves. Furthermore his poetry *seems* to conform to the stereotype that pupils are most likely to have acquired — that poetry should be spontaneous, sincere and direct, and poets young, passionate and anti-establishmentarian. The stereotype derives from the last century when Shelley and Keats had come to seem the quintessential poets, and it coincides with the revaluation of the Classics that preferred the 'spontaneous' Greeks to the 'artificial' Romans. Virgil then entered a period of semi-eclipse so that he can still be dismissed by a highly educated layman as a 'cold-hearted bore'; while Horace to many generations was an insincere, sycophantic embellisher of platitudes without an ounce of real poetry in him.

All this has changed at the scholarly level, thanks to Eliot, Empson and other influential poet-critics, but, outside academic circles, pop lyrics, the reverence paid to child poetry and child art, the pervasive fashion for breezy journalism and the cult of gut-reaction ensure that the *Odes* and the *Aeneid* do not at first seem like poetry to the fifth-former.

3 The antiquarian background and the commentaries

Not only were the members of the audience for whom the Roman poet wrote sophisticated, they were also contemporaries: he could naturally assume in them a familiarity not only with the prevailing literary conventions, but also with the happenings and the furniture of the world they shared. The present-day pupil does not see citizens of his town being carried round in *lecticae* or reeling home drunk by the light of flaming torches carried by slaves; nor can he glimpse Soracte from his front door; nor would he, if he escaped from a yachting disaster, hang up his clothes or any other ex voto in a nearby chapel; nor does he live under a dictator who is trying to restore the morals and piety of his fellow citizens by legislation, propaganda and example. The pupil reading Catullus, Horace or Propertius has to be aware of such happenings and furniture if their poems are not to be meaningless to him; he also needs to know the myths and legends which the poets allusively exploit. He will find no lack of willingness on the part of commentators to help him. T. E. Page's *elementary* edition of *Aeneid* I contains two full pages of notes on the first nine lines, only a few of which are to give assistance with the Latin. This is trifling by comparison with the ten pages devoted by Priscian to the first line alone, but it is enough to disabuse a pupil of any notion that he is about to read a fast moving story.

What should a good commentary do for its readers? One thing it should do, but only too often does not, is to show the reader why the text is thought to be worth reading; otherwise he cannot be blamed for concluding that classical scholars tackle their authors, like mountain climbers, simply because, after twenty centuries, they are still there. Where the Victorian commentaries did attempt this, it was, more often than not, by simply *exclaiming* on the excellences of the author or the beauty of this or that passage. The effect of this sort of behaviour, whether on the part of the commentator or the teacher, is to arouse in the pupil the enthusiasm of Mary Jane on being told that there is lovely rice pudding for dinner again.

The modern pupil is likely to have had far less time to spend learning Latin or Greek than his Victorian predecessor, so help with the difficulties of language, to a degree that stern pedagogues of the past would have called spoon-feeding, is desirable; but when it comes to antiquarian, historical and mythological information it might be better if the commentator asked himself how *little* he *need* give, rather than how *much* he *could* give. He might consider Eliot's *Waste Land* and its learned annotations, and the disclaimer of Ezra Pound, who was the poem's midwife, that any of the knowledge contained in them was necessary for understanding the poem. None the less, some antiquarian information will be necessary, and it is important that it be conveyed, by teacher or commentary, as simply and unobtrusively as possible; otherwise reading classical poetry will too closely resemble a museum visit to be any sort of literary experience.

Perhaps we should be talking of a new type of commentator rather than a new type of commentary. It was until recently a very vexed question in academic circles whether literary appreciation was the proper business of the classical scholar. A. E. Housman notoriously thought it was not. A group of scholars teaching in American and Canadian universities (some of them English by birth or training) who founded and contribute to the periodical *Arion*, are very emphatic that it is. They consider that the failure of leading British scholars (whom they sometimes refer to as 'the philological establishment') to add to their philological erudition the skills of a literary critic has had a seriously damaging effect on the reputation of Classics as a humane study. The 'philological establishment' retorted by scorning the literary critics as amateurs dabbling in meaningless judgments, based on inadequate linguistic scholarship. The truth is that both linguistic scholarship and the true critic's insights and love of poetry — modern as well as ancient, European as well as English — are necessary to produce illuminating criticism; but, as we have already accumulated a great capital of philological erudition, the fostering of literary sensibility among our scholars is the more pressing need.

The paradox

The concept of 'teaching literature' *is* a paradox. It is self-evident that literature is not composed to be 'taught'. It is composed on the assumption that there will be readers — or listeners — who will be induced to begin reading by the expectation of intrinsic pleasure or intrinsic profit or most likely both, and will continue to read because this expectation is being satisfied. Later, of course, the work of literature may join the 'hundred great books of the world', and readers may conscientiously plough through it to become educated, or to pass an examination, or to impress their acquaintances, or to extract information — sociological, historical, aesthetic or linguistic; but to teach pupils to read for any of these purposes is not teaching literature. Teaching literature implies teaching pupils to read literature as it was written to be read — with profit and enjoyment. It may be thought that trying to teach people to take enjoyment in something they do not naturally like is as futile as trying to teach a liking for new kinds of food. People, the argument would run, should be left to enjoy what they like. *De gustibus.* . . .

But people can be, and have been, taught to acquire new tastes in food, in time of famine or for someone's commercial profit. Many children from culturally deprived backgrounds would never, without help, learn to enjoy any poetry, even in their own language; but with skilled teaching do learn. Even for the literate, the enjoyment of *Latin* poetry is an acquired taste. Only after twenty years did Kipling find pleasure in Horace: many of his schoolfellows probably never.

In part it is a question of perception. Without help we look but do not see, as in those clever pictures used by experimental psychologists which seem nothing but a confused mass of formless smudges until one is shown that they conceal a human face; whereafter one can never see the picture without seeing the face. Yet it is not as simple as that, because of the ambiguity of art. What there is to see in a poem is fluid, and depends on what the reader brings to it in the way of experience both of literature and of life, so that no one can truly see what is in a poem through another's eyes; he can only be helped to see it through his own. But the first step is to persuade him to look at the poem long enough to see anything at all.

Towards a solution of the problems

There can never be a complete solution. Reading a poem in Greek or Latin can never be quite the same as reading a poem composed in one's mother tongue; but there are compensations. The language and its overtones cannot be staled by the clever exploitation of advertising copywriters; nor can semantic shifts (not infrequent with the vocabulary of Shakespeare or Milton) be a cause of misunderstanding. The exotic ambience, even the initial difficulty, can give an added flavour to the pleasure, and, once mastered, the difficulties do not recur at each reading. But it would be unrealistic to base a rationale of Classics teaching on the supposition that many pupils are in later life going to adventure by themselves into hitherto unencountered passages of Greek or Latin poetry. One can, however, hope that they may return to what they already know and love. The first step is to dispose of the doctrine of W. G. Clarke that the reading of Greek and Latin literature should be treated as *essentially* different from reading English literature. If literature is to be understood as literature, the ability to follow the story or argument of a poem and appreciate the subtlety with which it is presented is as important as to be able to articulate the language in which it is embodied. Since the publication of the Cambridge Latin Course it has been realized that this ability, in relation to Latin (or Greek) texts, can and must be taught from the start. If experience has taught the pupil that a passage of Latin or Greek is mere material for a decoding exercise in which the message to be decoded is at best trivial, at worst meaningless, then he will acquire an attitude of mind and habits of procedure that will persist when he is invited to tackle Caesar, Virgil, Xenophon or Homer.

Now that responsibility for initiating the pupil's ability to read Greek and Latin literature in the wider sense has devolved on the course writer, his task has begun to look highly arduous and complicated; and so it is. Not only must he write to a rigidly controlled linguistic schema, and situate his stories in a well-researched social context, but he must also put them together with a degree of narrative skill, characterization and plotting, capable of engaging the pupil's concentrated interest, and challenging his powers of moral and aesthetic discrimination, and exacting his critical respect. The plots and characterization must touch the pupil near enough to his own experience to evoke some degree of raw emotional response: yet they must not be twentieth-century plots and characters in thin disguise, but constitute a cultural introduction to the alienness of the ancient world. To expect that all these requirements shall be met with total success is to ask the impossible, but even moderate success will take us a long way further than those tedious narratives about *Marcus, puer Romanus* and *Virginia, puella Romana*, their Cook's tours round the *Forum Romanum* and the *Campus Martius*, and their frigid conversations about the heroes of Early Rome: and then those ruthlessly eviscerated stories from Livy, which place cardboard constructs like Menenius Agrippa, Cloelia or Mucius Scaevola, and such complex, legendary and fascinating characters as Scipio and Hannibal on the same plane of boring non-credibility.

Not all the responsibility devolves on the course writer. The teacher, too, must discharge tasks which he never bothered with before, if he is to develop the embryonic abilities of his pupils to see all there is to see in a piece of Latin, and consider it with discrimination. Negatively, he must not stand in the way of the course writer. If the narrative be 'acceptable but not predictable' (to borrow a phrase from a writer on the philosophy of history) the readers will want to find out what happened. They should not be frustrated by constant stops and starts imposed by the teacher. Boys learn from one another, or from TV commentators, to follow a game of football with increasing discrimination and attention to the finer points: there is no reason why they should not learn from a teacher to pick up the hints and cues which a good story-teller carefully plants as he goes along. In both cases the result is enhanced pleasure.

Literary appreciation

The classical teaching that most of us experienced being of the philological sort, a primary necessity is for the teacher to educate himself, and to go on educating himself, by cultivating his own literary enjoyment and discrimination. One cannot easily give to pupils what one does not have oneself. It has been said that an enthusiasm for classical poetry can only be caught, never taught. It can be caught – the literature of biography has many instances – but present-day conditions do not favour this. Nowadays it must be both taught and caught.

The literary appreciation lesson

Much has now been written about this, and a number of teaching anthologies have been published since the techniques were pioneered by Messrs Balme and Warman with their little book *Aestimanda* – a landmark in Classics teaching. There are differing opinions as to

whether, before operations begin, the text to be considered should:
1 be prepared by the pupils on their own;
2 be construed in class;
3 be read aloud by a pupil, or by the teacher;
4 be looked at alongside a model translation.

Whether any or all of these preliminaries are necessary or desirable will depend on the abilities and attainments of the pupils and the circumstances of the lesson. There are, however, arguments against (1) that the text may become a source of frustration, and therefore dislike, before ever the session begins. Against (2) it is argued that the process of decoding may be lengthy and its tedium jeopardize the liveliness and spontaneity of the later proceedings. In favour of (1) and (2) it can be said that it is dangerous (and dishonest) to discuss something which is imperfectly understood as regards its surface meaning, and the articulation of its language. However, some would say that comprehension and appreciation are properly inseparable; you cannot, or should not, try to understand a poem superficially and then dig down for profounder meanings. Against (4) it can be argued that the translation will, by its authority, pre-empt the pupils' own reactions and distort the discussion: and against (3) that the pupil will read the poem badly if he only half understands the sense of it. However, there seems to be no good argument against the teacher reading the poem at the beginning of the lesson (unless he reads badly — in which case he should learn to read better) while a pupil or several pupils read it at the end.

Conducting the discussion requires great skill and self-control on the part of the teacher. If he has done his homework he will have read and thought deeply about the poem; he is, anyhow, more experienced as a reader of literature, is more mature and has some first-hand knowledge of adult human emotions and human psychology which his pupils are only groping towards. His knowledge of the Graeco-Roman world is immensely greater than theirs. There are probably certain items of information which he has but they have not and are essential to the understanding of the poem. These must be given at once; but if the teacher is supplying too many clues to the understanding of the text, then the poem will remain a curiosity, too alien to have any significance for his pupils' lives. In this case the poem has been badly chosen, or the teacher is overplaying his role, or the previous training of the pupils has been inadequate.

What must at all costs be avoided is a style of teaching which makes it clear that the teacher knows precisely what the poem means and how it should be characterized, so that the discussion consists in the pupils guessing what the teacher wants them to say and being commended when they are 'getting warm', ignored or rebuffed when their guesses go wide of the mark. Such mind-reading exercises not infrequently go on when a teacher thinks he is conducting a 'free-discussion' — not only in Classics lessons.

For the discussion to perform its function, the replies to the teacher's questions must be sincere, and so must any statements that the pupils themselves volunteer. It is far more vital that they should be sincere than that they should be intelligent, let alone brilliant. If the teacher is not genuinely interested in what his pupils – all his pupils – are thinking, even when they are demonstrably on the wrong track, then they have no incentive to offer their opinions and there will be no discussion. A foolish opinion, if sincere, can lead to a useful discussion of what gave rise to it and why it is untenable. In the early stages of literary appreciation the teacher may have to let the discussion ramble freely so that the shyer members of the class can acquire the habit of talking. Later he will have to use all his skill unobtrusively to guide the discussion towards the considerations that are most crucial to the understanding of the poem.

It is possible to teach literary appreciation well in a variety of styles. These include, at one extreme, the fully permissive style. This allows the discussion to meander round and round the poem, so that any idea is pursued until it has become obvious that it is going to yield no further illumination; the teacher meanwhile contributes only questions and forbears to indicate whether he thinks a contribution perceptive and helpful or obtuse and irrelevant. The lesson comes to an end when the bell rings, and there is no attempt to draw any conclusions. At the other extreme the lesson is masterfully conducted by the teacher, who wants a number of items established (through the pupil's thinking, not his own) such as: the tone of the poem, its shape, diction and intention; the effects of sound and rhythm; the implied relationships between the characters in the poem; the view of himself that the poet is projecting; the story or dramatic setting; the contribution of metaphor, allegory or myth; the *chose vue* or how you could turn the poem into a film scenario. Every contribution offered to the discussion has to be substantiated by reference to the text, and by the end of the lesson a general assessment of the poem has been reached, from which pupils are free to differ, but do so with an awareness of all the aspects from which the poem can be regarded. This type of lesson requires a brisk and resourceful teacher and pupils who have been taught to stand up for themselves in argument and not to be over-impressed by the teacher's authority. The first type of lesson requires articulate pupils who have some experience of intelligent discussion. I have seen good lessons in both styles. The only rules for a good lesson are that all honest opinions must be treated with respect, the text under consideration must be kept in sight throughout the discussions, and be shown to have the power of touching on the pupils' own emotional experience. The lesson is not necessarily a failure because the pupils remain unconvinced that the poem is enjoyable, effective or significant. The experience of considering the poem may lead to a response delayed for months, or a year or more, or merely to a heightened ability to appreciate other poems. The rewards of literary appreciation should be cumulative.

Literary appreciation or literary criticism?

Aestimanda has been followed by a number of anthologies of texts, equipped with batteries of questions designed to teach Literary Criticism ('strengthening the critical muscles' is the phrase sometimes used). The traditions of Classics teaching being what they are, there is some danger in a tendency to turn a form of teaching designed to enable pupils to acquire a new source of enjoyment into yet another intellectual discipline, worthy of the ancient schools of grammar and rhetoric. For the teacher, these books are valuable in suggesting the sort of questions which might illuminate the passages chosen, but if the questions are put before the pupils as printed they are likely to inhibit the free and flexible conduct of the lesson by the teacher. The object of literary appreciation is not to turn pupils into precocious literary critics. Literary criticism, defined by T. S. Eliot and F. R. Leavis as 'the common pursuit of true judgment', seems to me to be essentially posterior to developed literary appreciation. It is a very intellectual exercise, dependent on wide reading and a deep love of literature. If practised by school pupils or immature undergraduates it could easily become priggish, cold-hearted and boring.

The author or the text?

In reaction against the biographical style of literary study, which seeks to illuminate the work of writers through research into their personal lives — a style which has had distinguished exponents such as our Hazlitt and the French critic Ste-Beuve — the 'new' criticism (so-called) adopted the slogan 'the words on the page', and considered it the critic's duty to discuss these and these only, without reference to extraneous matters. The poem was to be looked at as an autonomous object — a 'monument' or a 'well-wrought urn' — to the consideration of which the maker or the circumstances of the making are irrelevant. Furthermore the 'monument' is to be seen as significant solely by virtue of its artistry; attempts to use it to illuminate human problems are mistaken and doomed to failure.

However, it would seem that there is now some swing of the pendulum in academic circles, foreshadowed by our epigraph from Auerbach, towards a historicist interest in literature, which would make it a study in man's intellectual development. It is not a crude reversion to the 'personalist' fallacy attacked by critics from T. S. Eliot onwards:

it acknowledges the importance of interpreting texts through their structure, but regards this as incomplete without a further study of the relationship of that text to our European cultural tradition; a tradition which has now spilled itself over the whole civilized world. Such a programme would permit an extension of interest in a poem to the man who created it and the circumstances which moulded him; both the poem and the man providing a study in human potentiality and, inasmuch as we too are human, in our own potentiality.

Chapter five

On teaching Ancient History, Classical Civilization and Classics as a part of General Studies in the sixth form

The study of ancient history is in the last analysis not just the study of antiquity, and surely not of antiquities. It should serve to enrich the students' understanding of society, politics and culture in terms of, and in the interests of, their own experience and ultimately of the situations they will face in our society.

M. I. Finley

Historiography in depth — that is, methodical research into the historical growth of social as well as intellectual movements — is a thing unknown to antiquity.

Erich Auerbach

Preamble

Some justification is needed for treating the teaching of these subjects in the sixth form in a chapter of their own. There was a time, in the days when sixth forms were to be found only in grammar schools, when it was implicitly assumed that, during the six weeks between the end of a pupil's O-level year and the beginning of his sixth-form career, a mysterious maturation took place which made it possible and desirable to teach him in a quite different manner. This assumption was not as unreasonable as might at first appear. The ordeal of O-level had — and perhaps still has — something of the psychological effect of a *rite de passage*, and those who surmounted it successfully and returned to school for a further two years did so with the feeling that they were a select few, destined for university and dedicated for at least five years to the rigours and rewards of academic study. With the transformation of many grammar schools into comprehensives and a great increase in the number of pupils remaining at school after sixteen, and the consequent increase in the size of sixth-form teaching groups, the distinction between teaching classes of sixteen-year-olds and classes of seventeen-year-olds is nothing like as great as it was. None the less, attaining O-level and CSE — or whatever combined examination may be substituted for these — and, in the case of some pupils, the transference from a high school to a sixth-form college — is likely for the foreseeable future to mark an important stage in educational development.

Ancient History

For the purpose of clarity we may, perhaps, be permitted to behave arbitrarily and *assume* the existence of an entity which we will call *old-style* Ancient History and then describe its antithesis which we will call *new-style* Ancient History. Our hypothetical entities have some basis in reality in that, in 1965, a new (JACT) Ancient History syllabus was created as the result of dissatisfaction with the existing syllabuses and with the teaching they promoted. Nevertheless, it is impossible, without distortion and injustice, to characterize as a prevailing style of teaching the sum of the activities of an unknown number of individual teachers, so our 'constructs' must be looked on as caricatures or idealizations (depending on the reader's own views) which do not fairly represent the work of any individual teacher or examining board.

Ancient History — old style

This sees Ancient History as a humble but necessary ancillary to the teaching of the classical languages and literatures. It is impossible, the argument would run, to fully appreciate Greek and Roman literature unless the pupil has some knowledge of the outline of events which took place in Greece or at Rome before and during the times when the literatures were composed. The pupil needs to have in mind a skeleton outline covering the period from Solon to the death of Alexander, and then from the First Punic War to the death of Domitian. This narrative would cover the main political and military events. As the objective is a knowledge of facts and dates, the course can most economically be taught by the dictation of notes. In so far as interpretation is required this can be taken by the pupil directly, or *via* the teacher, from Bury, Hammond, Scullard or the *Cambridge Ancient History* (supplemented, perhaps, from the teacher's own undergraduate notes). The syllabus is to be examined by questions such as: 'Why did the Athenians fail in their attempt to win a land empire in Greece between 461 and 446 BC?' In tackling such a question the candidate is expected to display a knowledge of the military operations and political activities of the Athenians and Spartans during these years, and to add a few generalizations about the limitations of sea power, Greek love of independence and the precarious balance between pro-Athenian democrats and anti-Athenian oligarchs in the cities which had come under Athenian control — generalizations which can be fairly easily memorized from the pages of Bury, Hammond or the *CAH*. A great advantage of *old-style* Ancient History in a world which believed in specialization and allocated seven periods a week to each A-level subject was that it made possible a course of studies (in a classical sixth form) consisting of eighteen periods a week for Latin and Greek, which were difficult, and three for Ancient History which was not.

Underlying assumptions of old-style Ancient History

It cannot be said that the *old-style* Ancient History implies any particular theory of the nature of history or of how historical understanding is acquired (perhaps for this reason it has been the target of the gibe that it is more ancient than history). This is not surprising since its objective is not historical understanding, but acquaintance with a narrative of political and military events between 600 and 323 BC and 264 BC and AD 96. The assumption is that this acquaintance will facilitate comprehension of Greek and Roman literature. This assumption has been attacked on the grounds that it leaves pupils with little appreciation of the conjectural nature of the evidence for large parts of this narrative, and, worse, habituates them to thinking in historical clichés about democracy, oligarchy, demagogy, senate, *nobiles* and so on. These clichés not only do not evoke in the pupil's mind any accurate conception of the reality for which the cliché is a label, but they often disguise from the pupil the fact that he has never had to ask himself what it was like to live in a Greek *polis* or to be a Roman *nobilis*, and that if he did he would have no basis on which to construct a reply. The Greek and Roman historians who used these clichés were writing for a readership which knew the realities from experience; we do not, and are only too likely to associate the clichés with inappropriate items drawn from our knowledge and experience of contemporary politics. The attack has gone as far as to suggest that ignorance would be a better state in which to approach Greek and Latin literature than false conceptions inducing an unjustified feeling of knowledge.

An argument often adduced in favour of *old-style* Ancient History is the importance of knowing that Solon came before Peisistratus and Cimon before Pericles, the Gracchi before Sulla, and Sulla before Cicero and Augustus. This importance is real (though easily exaggerated), but no greater than the importance of knowing that Athens is south-east of Thebes and north-east of Sparta, or that Corinth is at the head, not the mouth, of the Gulf of Corinth. Both the chronological and the spatial relationships can be taught diagrammatically, the one by a time-chart, the other (as it has long been taught) by an atlas or wall-map.

Ancient History — new style

This sees Ancient History as a sixth-form subject in its own right, entitled to a full complement of periods and worthy of study by pupils whose A-levels do not necessarily include Latin or Greek, and who may not have any knowledge of either language. It considers that the objectives should be the same as for any other period of history (though the nature of the content will be affected by certain peculiarities of Greek and Roman society and culture). What these objectives are is, of course, a matter of controversy among all teachers of History, but they would certainly include some understanding of: the interaction of economic, social, political and cultural forces in the period studied; the uniqueness of this period; the nature of historical evidence and the criteria for assessing it; and the logical coherence required of a historical narrative.

The implications of the *new-style* objectives are that economic and social aspects of antiquity should be included in the course, and also some study of the art, architecture and literature of the period. Inasmuch as understanding rather than mere knowledge of 'facts' is aimed at, the methods of learning require a much more active part to be played by the pupil, in discussion, in reading and in writing. Neither the views of the text-book nor the views of the teacher are to be presented as more than provisional statements of the truth. The pupil's reading should include some of the literature of the period, some of the epigraphical evidence where this is available, and he should — in the case of Athens, at least — take a look at some representative samples of contemporary art and architecture. Since much of the evidence for the history of the Graeco-Roman world is in the form of historical writing by ancient authors, some critical study of the theory and practice of these authors will be an important part of the course. A suitable examination question might be: 'How much did religious belief and sentiment affect the course of the Peloponnesian War?' A good answer would be expected to show some understanding of the religious attitudes of fifth-century Greeks and to include references to plays of Aristophanes, to Plutarch's *Lives* of Pericles and Alcibiades, and especially to Thucydides. A statement such as that in Hammond's *History of Greece*, p. 435, that 'Cleon's use of oracles was a part of his plan to exploit the reaction against the new ideas and discredit his political opponents', would not be quoted without critical discussion about the reasoning that could justify such a statement.

Obviously a programme of this sort is possible only if the period set is (a) short enough to be studied, in all the aspects mentioned, within the time available (this means that it must be a period of 75—100 years at the most), and (b) reasonably rich in surviving literature. In effect these two conditions restrict the possibilities to the fifth and fourth centuries BC for Greece, and the first centuries BC and AD for Rome.

Underlying assumptions of new-style Ancient History

W. H. Burston, in his *Handbook for History Teachers*, recognizes three views of History (as an educational subject):
1 The developmental view. History is the past unrolled for the benefit of the pupil so that he can see the seeds sown in the past developing into the flowering civilization that he must live in and will thereby understand better.
2 The past as contrast. Intensive study of selected periods of the past is undertaken so that they may be understood in their alien essence, and the pupil may thereby receive a valuable counterbalance to the formative influences of the all too present norms of his own culture. (This is a milder version of the therapeutic culture shock advocated by sociologists in courses which show an eskimo child beating a seagull to death with the encouragement of his parents.)
3 The use of History for the teaching of general laws of economic, political and social behaviour, by virtue of which the pupil may learn to foresee future change.
The first two of these views are familiar to Classics teachers seeking a justification for teaching their subject in the twentieth century. The third view is familiar from the introduction by Thucydides to his *History*, but his version of the theory rests on the assumption that human nature is unchanging and, in effect, that we all live in a Greek *polis*. The modern version posits certain laws or, at least, patterns of social or economic organization which can be educed from a study of the functioning of societies in present and past time — with a preference for studying present time. Alternatively, it is based on a deterministic theory of evolutionary or cyclical development of the course of life on earth, such as Marxist evolutionary determinism, or Arnold Toynbee's theory of the rise and decay of civilizations.
The new style in Ancient History teaching, though it shows more interest in sociological theory than the old style (it would be impossible to show less), is closest to the second of these theories. It aims to study the unique and (to us) alien nature of the periods chosen, and to recreate them in their own right, rather than show their relation to modern phenomena. (The latter aim is more convincingly claimed by Classical Civilization courses.)

Criticisms of the old and new styles of Ancient History

Old style: Criticism here is scarcely necessary, as from the description it can be seen that it is not History in any serious sense, but a sort of general knowledge about the Ancient World, useful to the reading of, for example, Shakespeare's Roman plays, or for picking up references in art and literature in the same way that an acquaintance with the Greek myths is helpful. For pupils who were studying Latin and Greek in the sixth form and later at university its superficiality was, in most cases, greatly mitigated by the close reading of the ancient historians themselves that A-level and university courses in Classics entailed. As a study in its own right it has little to recommend it.

New style: There are two important criticisms. First, there is a paradox about the objectives of the *new-style* syllabus. It has been stated that it aims to study the interaction of the economic, social and cultural with the political aspects of a period. Unfortunately neither the Greeks nor the Romans wrote economic, social or cultural history, but they did write political and military history of high literary interest. To study fifth-century Greece or first-century Rome without reading Herodotus, Thucydides and Sallust would be to throw away one of the main arguments for the subject; but these authors will direct the interest of the pupil to the political and military excitements — very rousing and stimulating too — of the periods. The social and cultural history can only be educed from a scholar's knowledge of all the surviving literature, together with the archaeological and epigraphical evidence and a specialist's acquaintance with surviving works of art, most of which are in Greece or scattered among the world's great museums, and so unavailable to the school pupil. Therefore, it is argued, the pupil is still dependent on the text-book for forming his judgments. There is a further, more sophisticated, objection which arises from our paradox. Erich Auerbach in *Mimesis*, from which the second of the quotations at the head of this chapter is taken, argues that for social and stylistic reasons the ancient historians were incapable of formulating those organizing concepts (like 'Capitalism' or 'Romanticism') which are the stuff of modern historical analysis. Therefore the student will always (and especially if his studies direct him to reading the ancient historians) emerge from a study of Ancient History conceptually naive from lack of experience of handling what Auerbach calls 'synthetic-dynamic concepts' and 'syntheses of characteristic data'. For this reason a syllabus which sets up to challenge comparison with modern history is courting defeat.

The paradox can be exaggerated. The writings of the ancient historians cannot be critically studied by sixth form pupils without help from modern scholars, so even on military and political aspects there is some need for the text-book — or rather text-books. A judicious prescription of sources that were not historical or political in their main intention can make it possible for the pupil to acquire some understanding of their relation to the political events of their time. Aristophanes' comedies, Euripides' tragedies, the letters of Cicero and some of Horace's odes are obvious examples. Modern methods of photographic reproduction make it possible to study sculpture, vase painting and even architecture without seeing the originals, provided that some examples of each medium can be seen in actuality — not impossible to most pupils who are within reach of London or a good provincial museum; and visiting Greece is a much less uncommon experience for a school pupil than it was.

The sophisticated objection is two-edged. A facile acquaintance with Auerbach's 'synthetic-dynamic concepts' is often the bane of A-level Modern History, leading to the manipulation of empty or half-understood formulas (every bit as uneducative as the clichés about demagogy and *nobiles*). Preservation from premature exposure to such concepts might be an argument in favour of Ancient as opposed to Modern History in the sixth form.

The second criticism is that *new-style* Ancient History is an élite subject, too difficult for all but very able pupils. This reputation seems to me to result from some confusion of thought. By comparison with *old-style* Ancient History it is certainly difficult; but, as we have shown, *old-style* Ancient History was, in terms of study required, a half-subject which made few intellectual demands on pupils whose gifts and training lay in linguistic skill. If Ancient History is to be a subject in its own right, it must be as exacting and stimulating and as *historical* as any other period of history. There is no reason why it should be *more* exacting (though it would be agreeable if it were more stimulating). If it is, that reveals errors on the part of those who draft the syllabus and write the examination papers. There is, however, a significant difference between Ancient and Modern History at A-level. It is not taught by professional historians. Schools with large classical departments may be able to appoint a classicist whose specialism is in Ancient History, but in most schools the teachers' main interest may be in language or literature. So there is a sense in which it is a subject for an élite of teachers — not for an élite of pupils.

Justification

If Ancient History is to be seen as independent of the study of Latin and Greek, what arguments are there for studying it in preference to other periods of history?

It would be rash to claim *superiority* over other periods, especially as it is a tenet of many modern historians that all periods of history are of equal value. However, one may suggest that it has certain special points of interest. A period which has at its heart some study of Herodotus and Thucydides (and, less cogently, Sallust, Tacitus, Plutarch and Suetonius) forms as good an introduction as any to the study of the nature of history and the problems of historiography and biography. Though the periods throw up many historical problems which can be handled only by an expert, there are, none the less, issues in the rise and fall of Athenian democracy and the collapse of the Roman Republic which are broadly comprehensible to a modern pupil of seventeen or eighteen, and were treated vividly and powerfully by contemporary writers. Into the discussion of these issues moralizing too easily enters — and has been present from the first treatment of them by contemporaries — but the exercise of separating moral thinking from historical thinking is intellectually stimulating and a training transferable to other areas where the temptations are more subtle, because more intimately related to the pupil's own emotions or self-interest. The issues and the personalities involved in the crises of the Ancient World have been incorporated into the thought of European society to such an extent that much literature, and much historical and philosophical writing, from the Middle Ages to the present day, is unintelligible without at least the knowledge conferred by *old-style* Ancient History.

Classical Civilization

Classical Studies, or Classical Civilization, courses in the sixth form were at one time thought by many classicists to be a dangerous importation from the USA. The danger, it was supposed, lay in the possibility that 'soft' and inferior courses in which the Ancient World was studied in translation would drive out 'rigorous' and superior courses in Latin and Greek. 'Rigour' is an emotive and ambiguous word in academic circles. It is sometimes applied quite simply to subjects which are 'convergent' as opposed to 'divergent' in the dichotomy invented by Liam Hudson; that is to say subjects which demand precision rather than imagination, subjects in which success is achieved by the elimination of all answers except the one right answer; by contrast with subjects in which success is achieved by the creation of fruitful but unverifiable hypotheses. For example, the sort of translation of a passage of Pindar that is expected in an unseen examination is strictly controlled by established knowledge of Pindaric linguistic usage in grammar, syntax and vocabulary, just as an exercise in bridge construction must be controlled by a knowledge of stresses and metal fatigue or else the student may end by constructing real bridges which

69

collapse when trains pass over them: but no bridges are going to collapse if a history student argues either for or against the proposition that the causes of the English Civil War were basically economic rather than political or religious; or if an English student proposes an unorthodox interpretation of a poem by John Donne. On this sort of reasoning English History and Sociology are soft subjects and so is any study of the Ancient World undertaken through translated texts. However, History and Sociology have their own sort of difficulty, and English is no longer thought to need the stiffening discipline of Anglo-Saxon. Classical Studies, if treated seriously, will make all the conceptual demands that are made by English, History and Sociology.

There are two specific objections to the establishment of Classical Civilization courses, first that they are redundant and second that, if not redundant, they are inherently unsatisfying. The argument that they are redundant comes from teachers who maintain that now there are Ancient History courses which embrace social and cultural history there is no need for anything that labels itself Classical Civilization, seeing that everything worth while that it could contain is already to be found in the Ancient History syllabus. Furthermore, the argument runs, it is misguided to study ancient literature and art otherwise than in an historical context. The second objection, which cannot be made to apply to the study of classical art, is that literature cannot be properly studied in translation: to do so involves discussing other people's judgments since it is impossible legitimately to make any of one's own. Any defence of a Classical Civilization course has to begin by conceding that reading a literary text in translation is a different experience from reading a literary text in the foreign language in which it was composed; but that again is different from reading a literary text that was composed in one's own mother tongue – how different will depend on one's familiarity with the foreign language. The familiarity of fifth form or sixth form pupils with Latin and Greek is seldom great, so the reading of Greek and Latin literature in school is always likely to be retarded by linguistic difficulties. The single book of Homer or Virgil, the twenty or thirty chapters of Thucydides, Xenophon, Caesar, Livy or Tacitus, the solitary Greek tragedy or speech of Cicero – all read at the pace of thirty or forty lines at a stretch – give a very imperfect impression of the work and the author being studied. Reading an author in translation may in some respects be much closer to the experience of the author's contemporary readers. But this argument cannot be pushed too far. The catchphrase 'traduttore-traditore' – 'to translate is to traduce' – illustrates itself by the very difficulty of reproducing faithfully even such a simple two-word motto in another language. *No Smoking* notices, inscriptions and non-literary papyri do not lose much in translation, but with anything having pretensions to be literature there must be both loss and substitution: and in the case of lyric poetry, choral ode or epigram or even of prose passages where the author is exploiting to the maximum the peculiar resources of his language for conveying subtleties of meaning, then a translation is as much or as little use as a paraphrase.

What then of the literary element of a Classical Civilization course? Epic — the genuine epic of Homer, at least, if not the sophisticated epic of Virgil — Tragedy and Comedy and Didactic Poetry are all used as the vehicles of ideas which can be prized from their linguistic matrix and discussed for their intrinsic interest as well as for their place in the development of Western European culture.

The advantage of a Classical Civilization syllabus over an Ancient History syllabus on the one hand and a Greek Literature in Translation syllabus on the other is that it can be very flexible and allow a pupil and his teacher to develop interests in diverse aspects of ancient culture and in the transmission of that culture to the modern world *via* the Middle Ages and the Renaissance. Its disadvantage *vis-a-vis* Ancient History is that it disperses the pupil's studies instead of concentrating them on several aspects of one society in one period of its history, and so giving them greater depth.

The criticism that has been levelled at the JACT A-level Classical Civilization syllabus is that it is too difficult. It is possible that the amount of required reading is too great — experience will show — but to say that the specimen questions asked are more suitable for an undergraduate is to misunderstand the nature of an open-ended examination question. To ask what the *Oedipus Tyrannus* is about is a suitable way to probe an undergraduate's critical intelligence and the degree of attention with which he has read the play; and this is not disproved by Professor Dodds's contention that when he was examining at Oxford twenty or thirty years ago most undergraduates came up with some pretty implausible answers. The educated public is likely to gain most from a discussion of this vexed subject conducted by Professor Dodds himself with other scholars of a similar calibre, but the undergraduate, in formulating an unsatisfactory answer, can still reveal critical sensitivity and insight, and so at a lower level could a sixth form pupil who had studied the play in translation under a teacher who had taught him to think for himself within the limitations imposed by our knowledge of fifth-century Athenian society and its religious outlook and of the conventions of Greek drama. The question arises, Must the teacher himself be a Classics graduate and have studied the play in Greek? The obvious answer is, yes. The less obvious truth is that a Classics graduate who has studied the play as a linguistic and literary exercise may be less well-equipped to appreciate the function of the play as *stage drama*, than an English teacher who understands the dynamic functions of stage conventions in diverse cultures. Best of all might be a graduate of a university course in Classical Civilization who

71

had studied the play under a don who was both a classical scholar and an authority on the theatre.

The same question arises in the case of the philosophical element in a Classical Civilization syllabus, but here, significantly, most teachers would answer without much hesitation that a teacher competent in philosophical thinking would make a better job than a teacher who could read Greek but did not understand Plato's arguments. Similarly, historical sophistication is more important than the languages for the historiography syllabus. With the syllabuses in Epic, Comedy, and Satire the verdict might well go the other way. Happily, in Art and Architecture no dilemma occurs.

It is interesting to note that the Danish sixth-form colleges have a General Classics course which has been running since 1903, compulsory for pupils who are not doing Latin and Greek. One period a week is given to it for three years. Five books of Homer are read; some Herodotus; three dialogues of Plato; one play each of Aeschylus and Sophocles; a study of Cretan and Greek art. The course is examined orally, and there is also a system of course work marks. The course is alleged to be acceptable to pupils. A Danish teacher writes: 'The pupils generally seem to like the subject. Most appear interested, and we seldom have to cope with any aversion to the subject, as is often the case with religious instruction.'

The directions issued by the Danish Ministry of Education state:

The purpose of the instruction is to introduce the pupils to important aspects of ancient culture. This is mainly done by reading major works (or parts of major works) by Greek (Roman) authors, in translation, and also by studying works of Greek (Roman) art and architecture;

and in its guidance to teachers the Ministry recommends:

The General Classics course should always be taught on a documentary basis, i.e. so that the pupils always work with the text or a reproduction of the work of art in front of them. A systematic account of e.g. mythology, literary history, or art history should be given only when it serves and supports direct observation; the pupils should not be made to learn such accounts by rote.

The most important thing when studying the literary works is, above all, that the pupils are left with an impression of the human value of the works and their position in the historical development. Going into details (archaeological, historical, etc.) should only be done if doing so serves this main purpose. (Translation by Birte Jacobsen.)

Classics as part of a sixth form General Studies course

The contribution of a Classics teacher to such a course will naturally be much affected by the nature, objectives and organization of the course as a whole, over which he is unlikely to have much control.

One may summarize General Studies courses, very crudely, as follows:

1 Unconvincing gestures towards 'liberalism' by headmasters who, after they have inserted the specialist subjects into the timetable, and paired them with the ablest sixth form teachers, look round to see what is left of time and manpower for a course to which the available staff contribute whatever non-specialist offerings they can. Such courses are treated by the pupils with the contempt they deserve.

2 Courses designed by ambitious headmasters for ambitious pupils with an eye to General or Essay papers in Oxbridge scholarship examinations and to the interviews that follow them. These courses give a useful scope to Mr X's dilettante interest in analytical psychology or Mr Y's obsession with the strategy of the American Civil War, but they are still seen, by both teachers and pupils, as secondary to the specialist A-level courses, and they are approached in a somewhat functional manner which envisages the objective as essays or monologues designed to impress with knowledge rather than as the evocation of any continuing intellectual interest.

3 Courses in schools where the headmaster has a strong commitment to sixth form General Studies and where these are carefully planned by a carefully chosen team of teachers. Such a headmaster may have a serious conception of education based on a philosophical analysis of knowledge and intellectual development which makes him uneasy unless his pupils have some acquaintance with all modes of cognitive experience. He will be opposed to specialization in the middle school and insist that as an antidote to the necessary specialization in the sixth form there shall be an element of moral, mathematical, religious and aesthetic education (or whatever his favoured categories happen to be) available for those whose specialist programme is deficient in any of these.

This is not the place to discuss the realism or idealism of our three types of headmaster, but to consider what Classics can contribute, given a reasonably favourable opportunity. The possibilities are, of course, very considerable but will depend on the range of the Classics teacher's knowledge — or willingness to extend his knowledge. He could work on either of two opposite principles, offering a study of the decipherment of linear B or a project on ancient technology for the mathematicians and physicists and a course on Epic or Tragedy for the English specialists, or conversely Greek Tragedy for the physicists and mathematicians and ancient technology for the arts specialists; but in many schools he would need the talents of a virtuoso to evoke much response.

If more than intellectual titillation is to be achieved, some dynamic organizing principle is necessary, dynamic in that it touches on some latent interest in the pupils, strong enough to override their preoccupations with their academic rating. Psychological realism in *Medea* and *Hamlet*, or the anthropological roots of tragedy such as the importance of kinship and burial in *Antigone* and the divine right of kings in Beaumont and Fletcher's *Maid's Tragedy*: the largely overlooked cultural assumptions that work the plot in a Shakespearean tragedy being neatly illustrated by the justly famous account by the anthropologist Laura Bohannan of her attempt to tell the plot of *Hamlet* to elders of the Tiv tribe, who gravely rebuked her for her failure to understand that Gertrude had behaved correctly in immediately marrying her brother-in-law, that the ghost was an omen sent by witches, that Hamlet was bewitched by Claudius to become mad, that Ophelia was made mad and drowned by the witchcraft of Laertes so that he could repay his debts by selling her body to the witches . . . and so on, and so on: the moral being that one can 'misinterpret the universal by misunderstanding the particular'. The *Medea*, the *Antigone* and the *Bacchae* all have powerful themes which the brave teacher can use as catalysts to broach discussion of contemporary problems, but he must be prepared to leave the ancient world far behind if the discussion takes off, and to listen patiently to talk of drugs and sex and law-breaking and forget that he represents law and order and establishment values in the society of school. In a thriller by Amanda Cross called *The Theban Mystery* there is a fascinating fictional account of the *Antigone* being handled in this way in a sophisticated New York girls' school (Vietnam, patriotism, the draft and desertion being themes more vivid to the girls and their brothers than we in England can easily imagine). From this unlikely source teachers could derive valuable ideas on techniques and procedures and much inspiration.

Myth, including legends and fairy stories, has obvious potentiality. Jung's ideas have been brilliantly presented and illustrated in *Man and his Symbols*, and these could easily arouse introspective, not to say narcissistic, interest; which would need disciplining by a comparison with the more down-to-earth anthropological theories of myth. If such courses were not to become a virtuoso solo by the teacher it would be essential to exact the contribution of papers by the pupils.

If an alliance can be struck with the RE department and the Art Department, the Rise of Christianity could appeal to the renascent interest among adolescents in religion, or religions — especially in the anti-establishment, brotherly-loving, unworldly and pacifistic cults of today, which have sufficient resemblance to primitive Christianity to make primitive Christianity and its relations with the State and with paganism more than objectively interesting. The Art Department is not essential to the team, but catacomb art and early Christian symbolism have a very direct fascination to pupils who are surfeited with words in their other subjects.

Finally, for the philosophically-minded Classics teacher, sixth-form General Studies offers a promising opportunity for introducing adolescents to philosophical discourse. It has been suggested that Plato's *Euthyphro* could be used economically and effectively to make this introduction.

Chapter six

Epilogue

. . . tamen usque recurret

Schools and universities have been in turmoil for fifteen years and are likely to continue that way for several years more. To predict where Classics teaching will be when the dust settles is wasted speculation: more important is to ensure that it continues to meet social needs while remaining true to itself. Remaining true to itself implies that teachers of Classics and their pupils chose their vocation or their studies from interest in Greek drama, Platonic thought, the Greek or Latin languages and literatures, and the desire to cultivate or communicate this interest; not because Classics is highly regarded as an intellectual discipline, confers social prestige or offers a refuge from the contemporary world in an embalmed and idealized past.

In the past fifteen years many changes have been initiated or accepted by Classics teachers, so that the tasks of a Classics teacher have been transformed. I will try to illustrate this transformation by describing an imaginary day in the life of a fictitious Classics teacher. Not quite imaginary and not quite fictitious, as the lessons are a conflation of many lessons I have seen and the teacher an amalgam of some four teachers I know well.

A day in the life of a Classics teacher

Our teacher works in a large mixed comprehensive, where he is head of the small Classics department. His first lesson of the day is Latin with a second form. This is their third term with the language, and they are doing an early stage of the Cambridge Latin Course. The passage, which they read aloud, listen to on tape, and interpret by question and answer, concerns Gaius Salvius Liberalis Nonnius Bassus, a Roman official serving in Britain in the reign of Domitian. He is not everyone's favourite character, and in today's passage he is found ordering the execution of a slave-worker in one of the imperial iron mines in Kent; the slave being too sickly for hard work and Salvius too business-efficiency-minded for compassion. However, this action is strictly illegal, and the executed slave has a son who attempts vengeance. He attacks Salvius as he lies sleeping in the nearby villa of one of his wealthy clients; but the attempt is foiled, and the outraged Salvius demands the execution of all the slaves of his client's household, on grounds of collusion. To handle this lesson effectively the teacher has to decide whether immediately to concentrate on the new linguistic forms introduced, or whether first to draw out the less explicit messages of the story — such as the character of Salvius and his professional concerns as the agent of an efficient but insecure despotism in a recently acquired and distant corner of the Empire. Then our teacher may want his class to consider the narrative technique employed — it is a story within a story — and what effect it would be likely to have on the listeners. Alternatively the teacher could decide to devote much of the lesson to a discussion of slavery, in which case his task will be to modify the automatic nature of his pupils' moral indignation and develop some understanding of the complexities of slave status. By reference to earlier episodes in the Course he can point out that relationships of affection, trust and intimacy could exist between master and slave; and that the custom of manumission offered a slave the prospect of a free, prosperous and respected old age. He might want to suggest that civilization and social justice were two incompatibles in the bad old days — say, before 1974 or thereabouts — and that of the many forms of human exploitation on which civilization has been founded, slavery, even if the most evil, has not always been the most cruel. 'Civilization as we know it is based upon all the despotisms, the cruelties, the exclusions, the monopolies and the rapacities of the past.' So wrote a character in a Henry James novel about the social conflicts of Victorian England. Our teacher will not quote Henry James to his Form 2, but he might try to give them some idea that the world is not quite so full of simple problems crying out for simple solutions as they might think. No matter which way he decides to handle his lesson, it will require skilful questioning; and for this he must understand his pupils and they must have confidence in him. Ideally, it will require also rather more knowledge of social and legal aspects of Imperial Rome than he possesses, and he feels vulnerable to the unpredictable and probing questions that he both hopes and fears to provoke.

His second lesson is Ancient History with three sixth formers. They have no Greek and scanty Latin and are doing the JACT History A-level syllabus. For the moment they are working on the Culture of Athens option. One of the group has written a brief essay on Athenian education in the fifth century. He quotes *The Clouds* as evidence, whereupon another member of the group objects that it is impossible to take seriously a play whose chief argument against progressive education is that it produces bony buttocks and large penises. The essayist does not see why a comedian who makes his audience laugh should be taken any less seriously than a tragedian who makes his audience cry. The second speaker complains that this is a typically sophistical style of arguing; whereupon the third member of the group wants to know what was so wrong about the sophists — who were, after all, merely exposing the contradictions inherent in a property-based, slave-owning society. This speaker is, in season and out, the school's leading Marxist-Leninist, and our teacher, who is none too strong on Marxist-Leninism, feels that things are fast slipping out of control; so he intervenes to recall the discussion to the dialectic of Aristophanes, whom, it transpires, the Marxist-Leninist has not yet found time to read. Not that he is thereby disqualified from damning him as a spokesman for the exploiting classes, as there is, he claims, a definitive assessment of the role of slavery in the class struggle in the ancient world to be found in the Marx-Engels correspondence of 1855, and this our teacher is strongly recommended to read at the earliest possible opportunity. The teacher repays this courtesy by recommending to the Marxist an equally early reading of *The Clouds*, not least because it is on the prescribed list for the examination. On that unedifying level of argument the lesson and the first half of the morning comes to an end. During break our hero has just time to snatch a mug of tea before he is accosted by an art teacher and by one of the English staff. They are both taking groups in Classical Studies and they need from him advice and some of the illustrative materials and reference-books that form part of his inadequate, though complicated, departmental requisition. He leads them to his stockroom, which serves also as his study, and while there takes the opportunity to remind himself of some of the variants of the Theseus-Ariadne legend. Then he goes to the school hall to take his own double period with a mixed-ability, first-year Classical Studies group. By exerting all the narrative skill at his command he just holds the group's attention as he tells of the drawing of lots, the voyage, the arrival in Crete, the infatuation of Ariadne, the entry into the labyrinth, the struggle with the minotaur, and the escape.

Discussion follows: what was so horrible about the minotaur, and what so terrifying about being trapped in the labyrinth? Then the pupils conjecture what Ariadne might have said to Theseus as she gave him the magic ball of thread, and how Theseus, in re-emerging victorious from the labyrinth, might have described his fight to Ariadne. This discussion has to be cut short. Three members of the group are mildly maladjusted, and have begun to provide a powerful counter-attraction to the death struggles of the minotaur. The minotaur may symbolize the ultimate in maladjustment, but he is too long dead to compete for the class's attention with the disturbed and disturbing psyches of three vigorous twelve-year-olds determined to disrupt the lesson. So the teacher sets the class to act the story. He has a vague feeling that if he understood more about Jungian theories of the value of hero-and-monster legends for liberating the young from their psychological hang-ups, this might help him to handle better a task for which he feels under-equipped. As the school hall comes less and less to evoke the illusion of Bronze Age Crete, and more and more to resemble the playground during a particularly boisterous breaktime, so our teacher reluctantly concludes that, somehow or other, he must get himself sent on the next available drama course.

Spare time in the lunch hour is spent in giving a slide show to foster the enthusiasm of his voluntary Greek group: one day he hopes it will produce one or two full-time Greek pupils, but that is only likely after they have taken their Latin O-levels.

The first afternoon period is a CSE class doing projects on Ancient Technology. One group is busy with triremes, another with the techniques of the Greek potter, a third are building a miniature ballista; while the least technologically minded group are working on the Daedalus legends and concocting eye-witness accounts of the fall of Icarus.

The double period which follows is with a Latin set doing *Aeneid* IV for O-level. The reformed examination includes appreciation questions, and, with this in mind, our teacher engages the class in a discussion of Dido's behaviour on learning that she is about to be deserted by Aeneas. Why is she described as raging like a Bacchanal through the streets of her city? Is this, perhaps, to cool the lively sympathy we feel for her; and to hint at the superiority of Aeneas, whose emotions are no less passionate but more under control? Since both are leaders and responsible for the well-being of their followers, ought not duty, however disagreeable, to come before passion?

There is no difficulty in persuading the pupils to talk. The girls, who are in a majority, are quick to nail Aeneas as a Male Chauvinist Pig, and our teacher has a hard time preventing Virgil's complex and ambivalent treatment of Dido from being grossly oversimplified. At times he is himself in danger of being classified as a Male Chauvinist Pig for attempting to defend Aeneas and his sense of duty. The pupils, boys as well as girls, are by nurture, if not by nature, far more akin to Dido than to Aeneas. Relaxed, friendly and impulsive, they balk at tasks which are disagreeable because they do not come easily to them. They have plenty to say that is intelligent and perceptive as well as much that is irrelevant; but what most exercises our teacher's skill and patience, is persuading them to master what the text *actually says*, instead of guessing at what they think it ought to be saying. Nevertheless, there is a gratifying liveliness about their response: even the quiet pupils participate occasionally. But there is one girl who says nothing. She is present merely in the flesh: in spirit she is still with her twenty-four-year-old Aeneas, the storms of urban stress and parental conflict having last night driven them, not for the first time, to the same cave – an under-furnished bedsitter in a Paddington basement.

So ends the school day, but not our teacher's work, which may be any of the routine administrative chores that fall to a head of department, or preparation for the next day's lessons, or marking, or writing reports; or it may be a hurried journey to join other members of his local Classics teachers' organization in planning activities, in conferring about new examinations or in meeting with some friendly and helpful scholar to discuss the teaching of one of the new Sixth Form syllabuses.

For a whole century Classics teaching was living on a dwindling capital and extended credit. In the 1960s, with the abolition of the Latin requirement at Oxford and Cambridge, with the expansion of the universities and the beginnings of comprehensivization in the secondary schools, old-style Classics went bankrupt. But the Greeks and Romans are still with us: on the television screen, in the theatre, in the colour supplements and in the classroom. Now that they are treated with less reverence they are more engaging, more interesting and more stimulating. New-style Classics has not yet fully taken shape. In the opinion of some it still contains too much of the old Classics, in the opinion of others too little. Though new-style Classics owes much to the collaboration and to the thinking of teachers in universities, the changes in the universities have been more spasmodic. But in some universities they have been very considerable, and in all universities there have been some changes. In particular the very wide range of specialist teaching and research that now goes on in a university means that the study of the Ancient World is becoming fragmented. Ancient History, Ancient Philosophy, Classical Archaeology are being drawn into the larger departments of History, Philosophy, Archaeology or Anthropology. In some new universities the study of classical literature goes on within a School of European Literature and in all universities the development of joint-degree courses has linked Classics with other departments. One of the most striking new developments is that of degree or half-degree courses in Classical Studies for undergraduates who come up to university with little or no knowledge of Latin or Greek. Some university teachers have wondered whether Classics departments as such may not disappear, to become a dozen or so little enclaves within other bigger departments or schools of study. This, I think, would be unfortunate. If there is a unity in Classics, as claimed in Wilamowitz's definition of classical philology quoted in our Prologue (as I believe there is), this needs to be embodied in institutional form if it is not to be lost sight of. . . . But here I am trespassing on matters that would be better discussed by a teacher in a university department of Classics.

In the first issue of *Didaskalos*, in 1963, Robert Bolgar wrote:

Two things emerge forcibly from any serious consideration of what one might call 'the Latin problem'. The first is that some considerable change in teaching method is inevitable if the subject is to survive. The second is that the majority of the profession — and particularly its older members — are bound to feel opposed to this change, which will demand great sacrifices on their part. We are faced, through no fault of our own, with a situation where our only alternative to hard work and hard thinking is to watch our subject dwindle till it disappears from the curriculum and leaves us stranded. The testing moment has arrived for classical studies. We must prove that they are fortifying, that they strengthen man's power to deal with the problems of life. We must prove their worth or see them perish.

Since 1963 there *has* been hard work and hard thinking. This little book has been able to do no more than sketch some of the thinking. The bibliographical chapter which follows is intended to help the student to explore more of the thinking and to do some thinking on his own behalf.

Further reading

Chapter 1 Prologue

The two great books on the early history of classical education are: H. I. Marrou, *A History of Education in Antiquity* (English translation by G. Lamb, Sheed & Ward, 1956), and R. R. Bolgar, *The Classical Heritage and its Beneficiaries* (Cambridge University Press, 1954). They are full of information admirably organized, replete with incidental wisdom and can be read for pleasure. Werner Jaeger, *Paideia: The Ideals of Greek Culture* (3 vols, New York, 1939–45) is the work of a great scholar and is often described as 'monumental'. It is not to everyone's taste, tending to vagueness and idealism where Marrou, over the same period, is down-to-earth and astringent. James Bowen, *A History of Western Education* (Methuen, 1972) is a straightforward account with up-to-date references. J. E. Sandys, *History of Classical Scholarship* (3rd edn, 3 vols, Cambridge University Press, 1921) covers some twenty-three centuries, is astonishingly readable for a work so comprehensive and is innocent of any theoretical framework or 'synthetic-dynamic concepts': it is a very 'classical' work. For the later periods R. M. Ogilvie, *Latin and Greek: a History of the Influence of the Classics on English Life from 1600 to 1918* (Routledge & Kegan Paul, 1964) is brilliant and stimulating but, by contrast, too schematic to reflect the realities of what he describes: however, well worth reading. M. L. Clarke, *Classical Education in Britain 1500–1900* (Cambridge University Press, 1959) is interestingly informative, but dry in style, as are his *Greek Studies in England 1700–1830* (University of London Press, 1945) and *Higher Education in the Ancient World* (Routledge & Kegan Paul, 1971). Gilbert Highet, *The Classical Tradition* (Oxford University Press, 1949) is full of fascinating gems of learning but often superficial and patronizing: a very good book to quarry from. Steven Runciman, *The Last Byzantine Renaissance* (Cambridge University Press, 1970), brief but very interesting, discusses the effects of a thousand years of classical Greek education on Byzantine civilization. Marrou, Bolgar and Ogilvie all contain observations relevant to any discussion of the place of Classics in modern education, but for a fairly systematic debate on the subject the student is referred to six articles in successive issues of *Didaskalos* (nos 1, 1 to 2, 3) by R. R. Bolgar, E. W. Kenney, M. McCrum, J. P. Sullivan, R. S. Peters and Martin and Margaret Thorpe: also to articles by T. B. L. Webster and others in JACT Pamphlet 1, *Robbins and the Classics* (1964). Many of these articles are discussed in an interesting unpublished MA thesis – K. Kilburn, 'A Philosophical Critique of Theories of a Classical Education' (University of London Institute of Education, 1973). This thesis argues that the *proper* justification for Classics in schools is that it initiates the pupil into the traditional categories of thought of Western civilization. Part of Kilburn's thesis is contained in his article 'The Need for Classics' in *Didaskalos* 5, 1 (1975). It is criticized by Richard Pring in the same issue. The article 'The Narrow-minded Linguist' by John Roberts and Mark Mortimer, to be found in *Didaskalos* 2, 2, is an impressive debate by two very intelligent champions of respectively 'new-style' and 'old-style' Classics (available as a reprint from JACT). J. E. Sharwood Smith, 'Classics Teaching: its Nature and Contribution to Education' in *University of London Institute of Education Bulletin* NS no. 20 (1970) has, at least, the merit of brevity.

The Wilamowitz quotation in the prologue is taken from M. R. P. McGuire, *Introduction to Classical Scholarship: a Syllabus and Bibliographical Guide* (Catholic University of America Press, rev. ed., 1961), an extremely useful handbook to all aspects of classical studies (though its brief section on school teaching is related to the American not the British scene). The source of the quotation is Wilamowitz's contribution to Gercke-Norden, *Einleitung in die Altertums-wissenschaft* (3rd ed., Leipzig, 1927) entitled 'Geschichte der Philologie'.

Chapter 2 Classical Studies

No mention was made in this chapter of the Cambridge School Classics Project's *Foundation Course* folders and Teacher's Handbook (Cambridge University Press, 1972 onwards), but this is a very important source of ideas, even for the teacher who does not propose to use the materials of the course with his pupils. The course is intelligently criticized by N. Whines in *Didaskalos* 3, 3 in an article entitled 'The CSCP Non-linguistic Course: a Critique'. Most of what has been written about Classical Studies is to be found in *Didaskalos*, but mention should be made of Schools Council: 'Humanities for the Young School Leaver: an Approach Through Classics' (HMSO, 1967). On the function of myth in education there are three Jungian articles by M. Marshak and one by

K. V. Moore in *Didaskalos* 2, 1; 2, 3; 3, 3; and 4, 1. *Didaskalos* 3, 3 also carries 'Anthropological Approaches to the Study of Myth' by M. E. Kenna. The article by James Britton in *Didaskalos* 2, 3 on the nature of myth and its importance for children (entitled 'Odysseus and Commuters') is brief and pregnant; it needs to be read, and pondered, more than once. Some of the ideas expressed in it reappear in his *Language and Learning* (Penguin, 1970). Both these will refer the reader to works by Langer, Cassirer, Frye and Malinowski where many of the seminal ideas on myth will be found. For a brief and simple introduction to the study of myth in general and Greek myths in particular the student might do worse than look at J. E. Sharwood Smith, *The Bride from the Sea* (Macmillan, 1973). Elizabeth Cook, *The Ordinary and the Fabulous* (Cambridge University Press, 1969) is widely and justly valued for its discussion of myths, legends and fairy tales, and how they can be best presented to children. G. S. Kirk, *The Nature of Greek Myths* (Penguin, 1974) is the latest, most thorough and comprehensive critique of theories of myth in relation to the Greek myths: by a distinguished classical scholar who writes lucidly and well for a lay readership, is very hard-headed, and has for some years made myths his special interest. He rejects universalistic theories of myth, but offers nothing very substantial in their place. The final chapter, 'From Myths to Philosophy', shows the author at his impressive best. M. Grant, *Roman Myths* (Penguin, 1973) is a much less closely written book, easier to read though less well written. It contains much valuable material to illustrate the conscious manipulation by the Roman aristocracy of their country's past in the furtherance of national and, more often, class interests. For the student wishing to take the study of myth seriously there is an admirable annotated (and sectionalized) bibliography: John Peradotto, *Classical Mythology* (American Philological Association, 1973 — available from JACT). On language and child development a student is bound sooner or later to be referred to L. S. Vygotsky, *Thought and Language* (MIT Press, Cambridge, Mass., 1962) and various works of Piaget. I find Piaget very hard to read with concentration and profit, but this is a damaging confession and perhaps it is right to recommend him. Jean Piaget, *The Child's Conception of the World* (Kegan Paul, 1929) has interesting discussions of examples of children's anthropomorphic ideas about the material world, which suggest why myth can offer them special opportunities for self-expression. *Play, Dreams, and Imitation in Childhood* (Heinemann, 1951) and *Language and Thought of the Child* (Routledge & Kegan Paul, 1959) are other obviously relevant works, even though they are largely concerned with children younger than secondary school age.

On 'group activity' there is an article by John Watts followed by a 'Footnote' by D. W. Taylor in *Didaskalos* 4, 1. John Watts's course book for teachers of English, *Interplay One*, is published by Longmans

(1972) and has some material and many ideas useful for Classical Studies. Michael Massey has written on project work in Classical Studies in *Didaskalos* 4, 3. On the value of talk in the classroom there is James Britton's contribution 'Talking to Learn' in *Language, the Learner and the School* (Penguin Papers in Education, 1969).

So to the CSE or O-level stage. G. F. Tingay, *From Caesar to the Saxons* (Longmans, 1969) is the standard classbook for Roman Britain, and 'Roman Britain in School' is the title of a suggestive short article by Norman Cook and David Johnston in *Didaskalos* 2, 2. 'Roman History and the Roman Coinage' by R. A. G. Carson and 'Greek Coins and Greek Civilisation' by John Barron (both well illustrated) are in *Didaskalos* 1, 3 and 2, 2 respectively and could be helpful. Two publications by the London Association of Classical Teachers, *Working Paper No. 2: Classical Studies in CSE* (1970) and *Roman Home Life* (rev. ed., 1970) are splendidly down-to-earth, and in *Didaskalos* 3, 1 both Leslie Churchill and Martin Forrest write usefully on Classical Studies and CSE, while Andrew Kilgour surveys the scene from a Scottish angle.

Finally, on museum visiting, Renée Marcouse, *Using Objects* (Van Nostrand Reinhold for the Schools Council, 1974) is brief, to the point, beautifully illustrated and gives titles for further reading.

Chapter 3 Classical languages

On general theory and on historical aspects three books in the Longmans Linguistics Library series are scholarly, readable and very informative: M. A. K. Halliday, A. McIntosh and P. D. Strevens, *The Linguistic Sciences and Language Teaching*; R. H. Robins, *General Linguistics: an Introductory Survey*; and R. H. Robins, *A Short History of Linguistics*. R. H. Robins was trained as a classicist and has written authoritatively (and readably) on *Ancient and Mediaeval Grammatical Theory in Europe* (Bell, 1951). He also contributed an interesting short article to *Didaskalos* 1, 2 on 'Ancient Grammarians and Modern Linguistics'. The Longmans books contain copious bibliographies and will refer the reader to the important works of de Saussure, Sapir and Bloomfield. A. Meillet, *Esquisse d'une histoire de la langue latine* (Paris, 1928) and *Aperçu d'une histoire de la langue grecque* (9th ed., Paris, 1965) and L. R. Palmer, *The Latin Language* (Faber, 1954) are scholarly, fascinating and unfashionable in attempting to relate the Greek and Latin languages to their cultural milieu.

On the Cambridge Latin Course and its linguistic theory John Wilkins's two articles in *Didaskalos* 3, 1 and 3, 2 entitled 'Teaching the Classical Languages: towards a Theory' are essential; so also are the Teacher's Handbooks to the course — which are published by Cambridge University Press (1970 onwards). There are articles on the teaching of the CLC by Malcolm Ricketts in *Didaskalos* 4, 1, and by Christine Taylor in *Didaskalos* 4, 2. It was attacked by N. C. Dexter in *Latin Teaching* XXXV, 1 (1973). Dexter's attack was answered by the present author in *Latin Teaching* XXXV, 2 (1975). Scant mention was made in my chapter 3 of *Ecce Romani*, an enterprising new course created by a group of hard-working Scottish teachers in the wake, or the shadow, of the CLC. It appeals to teachers who want innovation but cannot afford, or cannot take anything as radically new as, the CLC. *Ecce Romani* is published by Oliver and Boyd (1971).

Waldo Sweet wrote about his work in *Didaskalos* 2, 2, and appended a copious bibliography. *Latin: a Structural Approach* is published by the University of Michigan Press (1957) and *Artes Latinae* by Encyclopaedia Britannica Films Inc., Chicago (from 1966 onwards).

The best introduction to the work of Rouse is a short article in *Didaskalos* 1, 2 by F. R. Dale, who was closely associated with him. The authoritative books on the Direct Method are W. H. S. Jones, *Via Nova* (Cambridge University Press, 1915) and W. H. D. Rouse and R. B. Appleton, *Latin on the Direct Method* (University of London Press, 1925). Back numbers of *Latin Teaching* (the journal of the Association for the Reform of Latin Teaching) contain frequent short articles on aspects of Direct (or Oral) Method teaching; those by H. Loehry have been published by Centaur Books, Slough (1970) as *Notes on the Oral Method of Latin Teaching*. *Principia* and *Pseudolus Noster* by C. W. E. Peckett and A. R. Munday, the course books designed to be used on the Direct Method, are published by Wilding, Shrewsbury (1949 and 1950); they are reviewed by F. B. K. Dennis in *Didaskalos* 3, 1.

Didaskalos 2, 2 has several articles on various aspects of the teaching of Greek, and in 4, 2, G. Zuntz reviews a number of course books, English, American and German. His unfavourable comments on the McGill course are challenged in 4, 3 by its authors.

The authoritative books on the pronunciation of the classical languages are W. Sidney Allen, *Vox Latina* (Cambridge University Press, 1965) and the same author's *Vox Graeca* (Cambridge University Press, 1968). Allen has written in *Didaskalos* 1, 1 on the pronunciation of Latin, and in 2, 2 on the oral accentuation of Greek. His views on the latter are challenged by W. B. Stanford in 2, 3. Stanford's own book *The Sound of Greek* (Cambridge University Press, 1967) includes a recording. On the teaching of Latin verse reading there have been a number of articles in *Didaskalos* which have been collected into a reprint (Brink, Nussbaum, Brink and Coleman: *The Teaching of Scansion*) available from JACT. JACT have also published a useful little monograph by G. Nussbaum entitled *Reading Virgil* and Discourses Ltd, Tunbridge Wells, market an excellent tape (with commentary) by Nussbaum entitled *Ore Sonandum*.

There are a number of articles on prose composition in *Didaskalos*

1, 2 and a reasoned defence of composition by J. E. T. Brown appears in 2, 1. Reference to its value and place in Classics teaching can be found in the articles on a Theory of Classical Education in volumes 1 and 2.

Chapter 4 Classical literatures

I can think of no better starting point than the two articles by J. V. Muir: 'Some Books for Critics' in *Didaskalos* 2, 1, and 'The Study of Ancient Literature' in *Didaskalos* 4, 3. *Didaskalos* 2, 1 contains also important articles by J. P. Sullivan and Kenneth Quinn, and an excellent discussion by P. S. Doughty of the various procedures available to a teacher in handling the discussion of a literary text. In the same issue the authors of *Aestimanda* (Oxford University Press, 1965) (M. G. Balme and M. S. Warman) discuss some of the work done by their pupils on some of the exercises in their book. Of all the conferences organized by *Didaskalos* that on literary criticism and the teaching of Classics was the most ambitious and the most successful. It included practical demonstrations of teaching at sixth form and university level by two distinguished teachers, a brilliant paper on theories of literature by J. Prynne, and a discussion of Horace's Cleopatra Ode by Brooks Otis. It was well reported and the report is available from JACT.

In addition to the articles in 2, 1, *Didaskalos* published in 2, 2 an article on literary appreciation by Robert Coleman; and in 2, 3 an article on commentaries entitled 'The Commentator's Task' by Kenneth Quinn.

Students wishing to study the acknowledged source of inspiration of *Aestimanda* are referred to I. A. Richards, *Practical Criticism* (Routledge, 1935) and I. A. Richards, *How to Read a Page* (Norton, New York, 1942); and for a criticism of the 'new criticism' to Helen Gardner, *The Business of Criticism* (Oxford University Press, 1959) or − specifically in connection with classical authors − to Charles Segal, 'Ancient Texts and Modern Criticism' in *Arethusa* 1.1 (Autumn, 1968).

The standard text-book on literary theory is R. Wellek and A. Warren, *Theory of Literature* (Penguin, 1963), very succinct and comprehensive, with a copious bibliography. The major work on ancient critical theory is G. M. A. Grube, *The Greek and Roman Critics* (Methuen, 1965): a bit stodgy, like many major works, but full of meat. At the scholarly end of a list of books valuable for the study of Classical Literature should come Kenneth Quinn, *Latin Explorations*; the two collections of essays edited by J. P. Sullivan, *Essays on Roman Literature*, vol. i *Elegy and Lyric* and vol. ii *Satire*; David West, *Reading Horace* (Edinburgh University Press, 1967) and Gordon Williams, *The Third Book of Horace's Odes* (Oxford University Press, 1969), both of which immensely enhance the pleasure of reading Horace; as will a brilliant little article on Horace's Pyrrha Ode by Kenneth Quinn in *Arion* ii (1963). E. Fraenkel, *Horace* (Oxford University Press, 1959) is a large and useful quarry for erudition and scholarly judgments. All scholars refer to it, mostly with great respect. George Luck, *The Latin Love Elegy* (Methuen, 2nd ed., 1969) illuminates the genre from Catullus to Ovid, and Gordon Williams, *Tradition and Originality in Roman Poetry* (Oxford University Press, 1968) illuminates the whole field (there is a shortened version in paperback, *The Nature of Roman Poetry* (1970)), as does, in a more detailed, more traditional fashion, L. P. Wilkinson, *Golden Latin Artistry* (Cambridge University Press, 1963). The first of the *New Surveys in the Classics* (*Greece and Rome* in collaboration with JACT), *Virgil*, by R. Deryck Williams is the ideal bibliographical guide to modern interpretations of the *Aeneid, Georgics* and *Eclogues*. Brooks Otis, *Virgil: a Study in Civilized Poetry* (Oxford University Press, 1963) is justly described by Williams as 'a landmark in Virgilian studies' because of the freshness of its critical approach. At the pedagogic end of the list come D. G. Fratter, *Aere Perennius* (Macmillan, 1968), A. Verity, *Latin as Literature* (Macmillan, 1971) and C. Stace and P. V. Jones, *Stilus Artifex* (Cambridge University Press, 1972), all of them constructed more or less on the lines of *Aestimanda* (the best of them, *Latin as Literature*, is the most original). An interesting and capable unpublished M.A. thesis (A. J. Hoskins, 'The Accessibility of Classical Literature', University of London Institute of Education, 1974) discusses the difficulty of presenting classical literature to modern pupils and takes a number of texts to illustrate this and to suggest possible solutions. Much of this thesis is to be found in an article by Mrs Hoskins in *Didaskalos* 5, 2 (1976).

On comprehension there is an excellent *Didaskalos* article in 3, 3, by David Karsten. M. G. Balme, *Intellegenda* (Oxford University Press, 1970), is intended for an earlier stage of attainment than *Aestimanda*; *Scrutanda* (there seems no limit to the gerundives) by M. G. Balme and M. C. Greenstock (Oxford University Press, 1973) is for an earlier stage than *Intellegenda*; and Graham Tingay (ed.), *Comprehendite* for O-level candidates. In *Didaskalos* 4, 3 there is a review article by D. W. Taylor of M. G. Balme, *The Millionaire's Dinner Party* (Oxford University Press, 1973), a brilliantly successful adaptation of the *Cena Trimalchionis* to make a 'bridge' text for use with pupils who are not quite ready to tackle Latin authors neat.

One cannot complete a reading list for this chapter without mentioning two inspiring books by Erich Auerbach: *Mimesis* (Princeton University Press, 1953; Doubleday Anchor Books, 1957) and *Literary Language and its Public in Late Latin Antiquity and in the Middle Ages* (Routledge & Kegan Paul, 1965). *Mimesis* is sub-titled *The Representation of Reality in Western Literature* and moves from Homer to Virginia

Woolf. Only the first chapters are on the literature of the Ancient World, but the whole book is a revelation of the power of scholarly criticism to illuminate both literature and life. *Literary Language* is a supplement to *Mimesis*, dealing with the development of the vernacular literatures of Western Europe out of their classical antecedents. Any classicist whose faith in the value of his subject has begun to wilt from its lack of contemporary acclaim will receive inspiration from these works, and a renewed assurance that the study of classical antiquity is essential for a full understanding of our present civilization.

Chapter 5 Ancient History

Didaskalos 1, 3 was specially concerned with the teaching of Ancient History, and contains articles by M. I. Finley and others which describe the theory and genesis of the JACT Ancient History syllabus. *Didaskalos* 3, 1 contains the syllabus and papers for 1968 and a review of them by John Hart, in which he describes his own very intelligent procedures in teaching it. There are authoritative bibliographical articles in 3, 2 by P. A. Brunt on 'Modern Work on the Roman Revolution' and in 4, 1 by A. Andrewes on 'Modern Work on the History of Athens 478–403'. Two articles with a sociological slant in 3, 1 by H. W. Pleket and A. W. H. Adkins are concerned with the relevance to modern society of the study of the Ancient World. *Didaskalos* 5, 1 (1975) contained a controversial article, 'New Ways of Teaching Ancient History' by J. K. Davies. *Didaskalos* 5, 2 (1976) has a reply to this article by P. A. Brunt. JACT has a well-established Ancient History Bureau which issues bibliographies and teaching notes, and intermittently a useful broadsheet *Bureaucratica* containing reviews and brief articles.

On the philosophy of history a start could be made with the article by W. von Leyden in *Didaskalos* 1, 3, but E. H. Carr, *What is History?* (Penguin, 1964) is stimulating, readable and not overlong. R. G. Collingwood, *The Idea of History* (Clarendon Press, 1946) is very important and has some interesting chapters on Herodotus and Thucydides, about whom he makes some unexpected judgments. W. B. Gallie, *Philosophy and the Historical Understanding* (Chatto & Windus, 1964) is especially interesting on the function of narrative in History (the phrase quoted on p. 57 is taken from this book). W. H. Walsh, *An Introduction to Philosophy of History* (Hutchinson, 3rd ed., 1967) surveys the field and is lucidly and interestingly written.

On the ancient historians there is M. L. W. Laistner, *The Greater Roman Historians* (University of California Press, 1971); S. Usher, *The Historians of Greece and Rome* (Methuen, 1970) and M. I. Finley, *The Greek Historians* (Chatto & Windus, 1959), which consists of selected passages translated from Herodotus, Thucydides, Xenophon and

Further reading

Polybius, with a long and valuable introduction. A. D. Momigliano, *Studies in Historiography* (Penguin, 1974) is stimulating and readable as well as learned: the work of a master in the subject.

At the pedagogic level W. H. Burston and D. Thompson (eds), *Studies in the Nature and Teaching of History* (Routledge & Kegan Paul, 1967) is valuable to any teacher of Ancient History who wants to think about what he is doing and why. W. H. Burston and C. W. Green (eds), *The Handbook for History Teachers* (2nd ed., Methuen, 1972) deals with both the theoretical and the practical and has sections on Ancient History: most useful.

On teaching Classical Civilization at A-level there is as yet nothing, except two brief articles in the JACT bulletins nos 24 (November 1970) and 28 (March 1972). However, JACT has set up a Bureau to issue bibliographical material to members and to elicit brief articles and notes on teaching techniques. Doubtless there will be articles in *Didaskalos*, or elsewhere, within the next few years as experience accumulates.

On General Studies in the Sixth Form there is a good article by Michael Hinton in *Didaskalos* 3, 2. There is little written specifically on Classical contributions to General Studies, though the articles by Jacobsen, Stray, Farrington and Else in *Didaskalos* 2, 3 are relevant, and also that by Murray in 4, 2. The report of the *Didaskalos* conference on the subject (available from JACT) has some interesting contributions from Lord James and others.

On early Christianity and the pagan religions, there are good articles in *Didaskalos* 4, 1 and 4, 2 by de Ste Croix, Gordon and Wiles; and, on teaching about Christianity and paganism, the articles by Martin, de Ste Croix and Gordon provide valuable references for further reading on the subject. *Didaskalos* 5, 1 has an interesting article by Robin Barrow on teaching Philosophy through Plato in school and there is already the article by Farrington mentioned above.

For Tragedy there is the useful bibliographical survey in *New Surveys in the Classics No. 5, Greece and Rome* 1971 by T. B. L. Webster entitled 'Greek Tragedy'. H. D. F. Kitto, *Greek Tragedy: a Literary Study* (Methuen, 1961), and H. D. F. Kitto, *Form and Meaning in Drama* (Methuen, 1960), which discusses *Hamlet* as well as the *Oresteia, Philoctetes, Antigone* and *Ajax*, are obvious choices to stimulate discussion. The thriller mentioned on p. 74 – Amanda Cross, *The Theban Mystery* – was published by Gollancz in 1972. The story of *Hamlet* among the Tiv appeared in a third programme talk entitled 'Miching Mallecho' given in 1953 and published in John Morris (ed.), *From the Third Programme: a Ten-Years' Anthology* (Nonesuch Press, 1956). C. G. Jung and M. L. von Franz (eds), *Man and his Symbols* (on Jungian interpretations of myths, fairytales and art) is published by Aldus with W. H. Allen (1964).

Chapter 6 Epilogue

Didaskalos, 3, 2 has several articles on Classics in the universities. Others are to be found in 1, 3 (Ryder and Ogilvie – who has some important comments to make on postgraduate research), in 3, 1 (Davies and Moly-neux, Wilkinson), in 3, 3 (Kirk) and in 4, 1 – on Classical Studies as a degree course – by Peter Walcot. Classics at Warwick and Classics in universities in New Zealand are the subjects of articles by T. J. Winnifrith and John A. Barsby respectively in *Didaskalos* 5, 1 while in the very first issue of *Didaskalos* the late Martin Wight wrote on the place of Classics at Sussex University which, like Warwick, was founded without a Classics Department. The JACT Bulletin frequently carries a very brief university article, and those in nos 33 (November 1973) and 34 (March 1974) on Classics at Sussex and Warwick are perhaps of special interest. Of a factual nature is B. R. Rees (ed.), *Classics, an Outline for the Intending Student* (Routledge & Kegan Paul, 1970). E. R. Dodds, *Classical Teaching in an Altered Climate* (Murray, 1964) is a very sane Presidential Address to the Classical Association by one of the greatest living classical scholars. M. I. Finley, *The Use and Abuse of History* (Chatto & Windus, 1975) has a chapter entitled 'The Heritage of Isocrates' which is more controversial on the actuality and potentiality of Classics in the twentieth century. The author has been and still is immensely and justly influential in the rethinking of Classics teaching. M. R. P. McGuire, *Introduction to Classical Scholarship* (for details see p. 83), though already out of date, and written from an American angle, presents, very stimulatingly, much information about developing conceptions of how Classics should be properly studied in a university. He quotes J. E. Sandys (q.v. on p. 82) for a definition of Classics which has become inadequate through the extension of knowledge and interests: 'Classical scholarship may be described as being . . . the accurate study of the language, literature and art of Greece and Rome and of all they teach us as to the nature and history of man.' McGuire proposes the substitution of the following: 'Classical scholarship is the systematic study and investigation of Ancient Greek and Roman civilization in all its various manifestations as they are known to us through extant literary and archaeological remains, and of the civilizations of the Near East (Egypt, Syria and Palestine, Asia Minor and Mesopotamia) in so far as these civilizations influenced or were influenced by Greek and Roman civilization.'

Anyone wishing to study present trends in the universities might do well to look at inaugural lectures delivered by scholars recently appointed to university chairs of Latin or Greek or Classics. There have been a number of interesting and promising appointments in recent years.

Finally, of general pedagogic interest are the following:

Further reading

Ministry of Education, *Suggestions for the Teaching of Classics* (Pamphlet No. 37, HMSO, 1959). This has been updated to 1971 in a brief supplementary pamphlet entitled *Classics in the Curriculum* (available free from the Publications Officer, Department of Education and Science).
IAAM, *The Teaching of Classics* (Cambridge University Press, first published 1954, 2nd rev. ed., 1961). This is now very out of date in many respects but makes an interesting key to respectable thinking in the 1940s and 1950s. It is at the present time being completely rewritten.
Schools Council, *Working Paper No. 23, Teaching Classics Today* (HMSO, 1969). The Schools Council are also about to bring out a pamphlet on the teaching of Classical Studies, which should prove useful in many ways.

Periodicals

Didaskalos has been frequently referred to in this bibliographical survey. It has appeared annually and three issues make a volume. Volume 1 includes the issues for the years 1963–5, Volume 2 1966–8, Volume 3 1969–71, Volume 4 1972–4 and Volume 5 1975–7. It is published by Basil Blackwell, Oxford, for the Joint Association of Classical Teachers, whose address is 31–34 Gordon Square, London WC1H 0PY.
Greece and Rome is intended for teachers and sixth formers. It is published twice annually by the Clarendon Press, Oxford, for the Classical Association. In association with JACT it produces *New Surveys in the Classics* – valuable bibliographical surveys of recent work on Classical authors. To date *Virgil, Cicero, Homer, Tacitus, Greek Tragedy, Thucydides, Livy* and *Horace* have appeared. These are available from JACT.
Latin Teaching is the journal of the Association for the Reform of Latin Teaching. It contains articles about teaching Greek as well as Latin and for some time has not been exclusively concerned with Oral Method. It used to appear twice yearly, but has become somewhat irregular of late. Both *Didaskalos* and *Latin Teaching* are sent free to members of JACT.
Arion, Journal of the Humanities and the Classics contains articles of literary criticism and, occasionally, on aspects of Classics teaching. They are of wildly varying quality, but some very good indeed. It used to be published by the University of Texas, Austin, Texas quarterly (nominally, but in fact irregularly). Since 1973 a new series is published by the Department of University Professors, Boston University, Mass., USA. Vol. III, no. 4 (1964), in the Texas series, contains answers from Auden, Fitzgerald, Logue, Murdoch, Powell, Steiner, Updike *et al.* to a questionnaire on 'The classics and the man of letters': very interesting.

Finally four series of reasonably priced books that make a useful contribution to Classics teaching:

The Ancient Culture and Society Series (Chatto & Windus) edited by M. I. Finley, which is intended for the intelligent sixth former or under-graduate and, as its title suggests, assists the new orientation in Ancient History teaching.

The Inside the Ancient World Series (Macmillan) edited by M. R. F. Gunningham is intended for fifth or sixth formers in schools and is designed especially to stimulate class discussion.

The Greek and Roman Topics Series (Allen & Unwin), edited by Robin Barrow, is intended for the lower forms of the secondary school, and will lend itself to group and project work on the Ancient World. The series treats such basic social topics as Slavery, Work, Religion and Religious Buildings and Athletics.

Intended for the same age range is the Longman series Aspects of Roman Life and Aspects of Greek Life. The text is brief and set out for easy comprehension with simple questions to test recall and plenty of good illustrations. Supplementary folders containing source materials and worksheets are available for some of the titles in the series.

Students Library of Education

General Editor Lionel Elvin

The Foundations of Twentieth-Century Education. E. Eaglesham.
128 pp.
The French Influence on English Education. W. H. G. Armytage.
128 pp.
*The German Influence on English Education. W. H. G. Armytage.
142 pp.
Mediaeval Education and the Reformation. J. Lawson. 128 pp.
Recent Education from Local Sources. Malcolm Seaborne. 128 pp.
*The Russian Influence on English Education. W. H. G. Armytage.
138 pp.
Secondary School Reorganization in England and Wales. Alun
Griffiths. 128 pp.
Social Change and the Schools: 1918–1944. Gerald Bernbaum.
128 pp.
The Social Origins of English Education. Joan Simon. 132 pp.

PHILOSOPHY

Education and the Concept of Mental Health. John Wilson. 99 pp.
Indoctrination and Education. I. A. Snook. 128 pp.
Interest and Discipline in Education. P. S. Wilson. 142 pp.
The Logic of Education. P. H. Hirst and R. S. Peters. 196 pp.
Philosophy and the Teacher. Edited by D. I. Lloyd. 180 pp.
The Philosophy of Primary Education. R. F. Dearden. 208 pp.
Plato and Education. Robin Barrow. 96 pp.
Problems in Primary Education. R. F. Dearden. 160 pp.

PSYCHOLOGY

Creativity and Education. Hugh Lytton. 144 pp.
Group Study for Teachers. Elizabeth Richardson. 144 pp.
Human Learning: A Developmental Analysis. H. S. N. McFarland.
136 pp.
An Introduction to Educational Measurement. D. Pidgeon and A.
Yates. 122 pp.
Modern Educational Psychology: An Historical Introduction. E. G.
S. Evans. 118 pp.
An Outline of Piaget's Developmental Psychology. Ruth M. Beard.
144 pp.
Personality, Learning and Teaching. George D. Handley. 126 pp.
*Teacher Expectations and Pupil Learning. Roy Nash. 128 pp.
Teacher and Pupil: Some Socio-Psychological Aspects. Philip
Gammage. 128 pp.
Troublesome Children in Class. Irene E. Caspari. 160 pp.

SOCIOLOGY

Basic Readings in the Sociology of Education. D. F. Swift. 368 pp.
Class, Culture and the Curriculum. Denis Lawton. 140 pp.
Culture, Industrialisation and Education. G. H. Bantock. 108 pp.
*Education at Home and Abroad. Joseph Lauwerys and Graham Tayar. 144 pp.
Education, Work and Leisure. Harold Entwistle. 118 pp.
The Organization of Schooling: A Study of Educational Grouping Practices. Alfred Yates. 116 pp.
*Political Education in a Democracy. Harold Entwistle. 144 pp.
The Role of the Pupil. Barbara Calvert. 160 pp.
The Role of the Teacher. Eric Hoyle. 112 pp.
The Social Context of the School. S. John Eggleston. 128 pp.
The Sociology of Educational Ideas. Julia Evetts. 176 pp.

CURRICULUM STUDIES

*Towards a Compulsory Curriculum. J. P. White. 122 pp.

INTERDISCIPLINARY STUDIES

*Educational Theory: An Introduction. T. W. Moore. 116 pp.
Perspectives on Plowden. R. S. Peters. 116 pp.
*The Role of the Head. Edited by R. S. Peters. 136 pp.

* Library edition only